CHARACTER
of CHRIST

LEADING
TRANSFORMATION
THROUGH TRANSPARENCY,
ACCOUNTABILITY,
AND MENTORING

BOB RUSSELL
TIM WALLINGFORD
DAVID FAUST
ALAN AHLGRIM
LARRY TRAVIS

EDITED BY JEFFREY DERICO

COLLEGE
P R E S S

COLLEGE PRESS PUBLISHING COMPANY
Joplin, Missouri

ISBN 978-0-89900-268-2

Authors: Jeffrey Derico (editor), Alan Ahlgrim, David Faust, Bob Russell,
Larry Travis, Tim Wallingford

Scriptures reflect the New International Version unless otherwise noted.

TABLE OF CONTENTS

Scripture says it's up to every Christian to clarify the true gospel – to lay out for their family, friends, and neighbors the conditions that God requires for them to receive salvation. God also promises power to make us bold in persuading others (2 Corinthians 3:12). The Greek word for *bold* is *parresia*, meaning "to go public." It carries the idea of being free and uninhibited in speech. God commissions us to go public with the gospel. So, who is up to the task (2 Corinthians 2:16)? According to the apostle Paul, we are, recognizing that it is God who makes us competent for this ministry of reconciliation (2 Corinthians 3:6).

How does God make us competent to be his witness? Is there a training manual that teaches us how to reach our neighborhoods for Christ? Can we truly identify the barriers that keep our neighbors from salvation? Absolutely! It starts with every Christian adopting a new mission statement. It should read something like this: *Be like Jesus in character and mission.*

Today, the American Church struggles to transform believers into Christ's character and to engage the Body to execute Christ's mission. Instead of being transformed, many Christians are being conformed to the patterns of the world. As a result, the Church is having negligible impact in 21st century America.

For that reason, the *Center for Church Leadership has* undertaken the TRANSFORMATION PROJECT. Our authors are praying that God will use this book to enable Church leaders to revisit and restore the biblical mandate of sanctification because transformation authenticates the believer's salvation. It enables Christians to fulfill God's mission for their life. Finally, it produces healthy congregations and mobilizes the membership to reach their neighborhoods for Christ. The miracle of personal and church transformation gives our message authenticity and our witness credibility. We will have no impact and we fail to serve as the light of the world if we are not continually being changed into the image of God (2 Corinthians 5:17; Ephesians 5:1). *So, this book's entire purpose is dedicated to who, what, where, when and why of spiritual transformation.*

In Section One, Bob Russell addresses the heart of transformation by listing three essential shifts that cooperate with God's sanctifying process. Section Two is my contribution, in which I give reasons why believers are failing to be changed and outline the transformation process the apostle Paul describes in 2 Corinthians 3. In Section Three, David Faust shares the value of transparency and its foundational role in Christ-centered relationships that transform. A highly practical discussion of the importance and primary components of effective accountability are presented by Alan Ahlgrim in Section Four. Last but not least, Larry Travis uses Section Five to describe the power of a godly mentor and to provide testimonies from protégés that give powerful testimony to how God uses mentoring in the transformation process.

Application questions, written by Jeffrey Derico, are provided at the end of every chapter in an effort to prompt personal reflection, paradigm shifts, and changes in the ways you plan and execute your leadership – of yourself, your family, your congregation, and your neighbors. There are also group discussion questions at the end of each chapter that can be used by leadership teams to create dialogue, tear down silos, wrestle with core values, create shared meaning, build camaraderie, and discuss ways to enhance the systems and processes your church uses to promote and facilitate transformation.

In 2019, *The Center for Church Leadership* will focus on the second half of the believer's Mission Statement: Be like Jesus in…*mission*. But only when believers are being transformed into the image of Christ will they have the God-given passion to redeem their neighborhoods by being the hands, feet, eyes, ears and voice of Christ. So first things first. I pray that this book inspires, encourages, and empowers you to become more and more like Jesus in character.

TIM WALLINGFORD
DIRECTOR
CENTER FOR CHURCH LEADERSHIP

the HEART of TRANSFORMATION

BOB RUSSELL

CHAPTER 1

TRANSFORMED INTO HIS IMAGE: 1 PETER 1:13-2:3

The birth of a baby is almost always a time of great rejoicing. If I show you a picture of a new, eight-pound grandson you would be excited for me and probably complement his appearance. But that joy presupposes the normal growth of the child. On the other hand, if I show you a picture of a five-year old grandson who still weighs eight pounds and is not talking or walking, there would be sympathy, not joy. It's expected that a healthy baby will grow and be transformed from an infant into a child, and later into an adult. If that doesn't occur, something is seriously wrong and there will be disappointment rather than rejoicing.

1 Peter 1:13-2:3 emphasizes the same principle as it applies to us spiritually. There should be a maturing process that follows a new birth. This transformation is usually gradual, and over time we experience change as we assume the likeness of Christ. The opening paragraph of First Peter affirms that we have been born again and that we have received new life in Christ. But that is not the end of the story. The fact that verse 13 begins with, "Therefore" demands something more after we have been born again; there needs to be a maturing process. A transformation is expected to follow.

It's sad when people have been Christians for many years but yet there has been very little spiritual growth in their lives. They don't know much more about the Bible than when they first became a Christian. Their thinking is just as shallow and worldly as it ever was. Their behavior isn't much different than when they first came to know the Lord. There's not much distinctive about them other than they go to church two or three times a month. Their relationships are still pretty superficial. They've got some Christian friends but they are still much the same as they were before they gave their life to Christ. They have been reborn, but not transformed.

The Apostle Paul expressed frustration with the Corinthian Christians for their lack of spiritual development and transformation. He wrote, "I could not address you as people who live by the Spirit but as people who are still worldly—mere infants in Christ. I gave you milk, not solid food, for you were not yet ready for it. Indeed, you are still not ready" (1 Corinthians 3:1-2). In this letter, the Apostle Peter encourages his readers not to be stunted in their development but to move on to maturity in Christ. This complements the last phrase of 1 Peter 2:2 which reads, "Grow up in your salvation, now that you have tasted that the Lord is good."

When Glen Hedgspeth, a friend of mine, was a young boy, his father took the family out to eat at an exclusive restaurant. Glen, as young boys will do, ordered the same thing he always did when they went out to eat—a cheeseburger, fries and a Coke. His dad said, "Glen, I want you to try something different tonight. I'm going to order you a filet mignon. If you don't like it, I'll order you a cheeseburger." Glen agreed. The filet came to the table and he took a bite and chewed for just a moment. His eyes lit up. He exclaimed, "Dad, why didn't you tell me about this before?" This illustration reminds me that many believers choose to consume "hamburger" for every meal, even though there's so much more to the Christian life. They've been satisfied with having been saved. But salvation goes well beyond understanding the basics of the gospel. Simon Peter challenges us to taste the "filet mignon" of God's Word and see that He is good.

Stated another way, it isn't just about getting us into Heaven; it's about getting Heaven into us here. It's about being transformed and looking more like Jesus as the years go by. It's about having deep enough roots that we can withstand the storms of trouble and temptations that inevitably beat upon our lives. Let's look at three areas in which we need to be transformed so that we can experience the abundant life that God wants to give us—we need to be transformed mentally, morally, and relationally.

I. WE ARE TRANSFORMED MENTALLY – we grow
from being emotionally driven to Scripturally driven

"Therefore, prepare your minds for action; be self-controlled; set your hope fully on the grace to be given you when Jesus Christ is revealed" (v. 13). As a young man studying for ministry, I was taught that was the proper three-step progression of following Christ: facts, faith, and finally feelings. There are facts to be believed. There are commands to be obeyed by faith. And then there are feelings to be experienced as a result. That was understood to be the natural order.

But cultural values today emphasize emotion much more than thinking, and feelings often trump facts. For example, a Facebook post that's hilarious or touching will get many times more hits than an article that stimulates thought. Descriptions of the arts, politics, and entertainment are largely about feelings. "This movie will terrorize you!" "The beat of this song will energize you!" "This painting is not meant to depict anything in particular; the question is how do you feel when you look at it?" "I voted for that candidate because he's got so much charisma that he makes you feel confident in his leadership." "Take this drug and you'll feel so peaceful."

You've heard the popular slogans: "If it feels good, do it," "Follow your heart," "You've got to be true to yourself," "If the chemistry's right, go for it," and, "It can't be wrong because it feels so right." Justin Timberlake sings, "Can't stop the feeling!" which includes the lyrics, "I don't need no reason, don't need control. I fly so high, no ceiling, when I'm in my zone."

It is not surprising that many churches, in an attempt to relate to modern culture, also choose to emphasize emotions over facts. Some Christian teachers speak more often about God's "inner guidance" than they do about the absolutes of God's Word. It seems to me there are more "Hold me close" songs than "What we believe" songs. A great deal of attention is given to lighting, staging, and fog machines in order to create a spiritual mood in church auditoriums. Preachers and worship leaders evaluate services more by what is felt than what is taught. My brother John retired from a forty-year ministry about seven years ago. After mentoring a group of young ministers he quipped, "If I hear one more young preacher say, 'That service lacked energy,' I'm going to throw up."

Please don't misunderstand; excitement, fear, laughter, joy, sadness, grief, anger, and romance are all Biblical and proper. Emotions are God-given and healthy. We're commanded in Scripture to love God with all our hearts. Solomon said there is a time to weep and a time to laugh (Ecclesiastes 3:4). God was pleased when King David was so excited about the Ark of the Covenant returning to Jerusalem that he danced for joy in front of the parade (2 Samuel 6:14).

But God has also given us the capacity to think. "'Come now and let us reason together,' saith the Lord…" (Isaiah 1:18; KJV). We're commanded to love God with all our minds (Mark 12:30), to be "transformed by the renewing of your mind" (Romans 12:2), to "have the same mindset as Jesus Christ" (Philippians 2:5), and "to prepare our minds for action" (1 Peter 1:13).

Feelings are valuable but reason is more important and should therefore be given priority. Feelings fluctuate. They aren't dependable. What elicits strong emotion in your heart today can leave you unmoved next week. But facts remain a solid foundation of faith and obedience.

W.A. Criswell, a famous Southern Baptist preacher, once quipped after fifty years of marriage, "Sometimes I loved my wife so much I could just eat her up. Then the next day, I wish I had!" He went on to teach that if your marriage is based solely on emotion, it's on shaky ground.

As we mature in the Christian life and become transformed into the image of Christ, we should move from being emotionally-driven to Scripturally-driven. You might expect me to say rationally-driven but reason is not a sufficient foundation either. The Bible says, "There is a way that appears to be right, but in the end it leads to death" (Proverbs 14:12).

Mature followers of Christ saturate their minds with God's Word until it comes out their pores. They condition their minds to respond according to God's commands regardless of how they feel about them at the moment. They develop a submissive spirit toward God's directives much like an Army private is conditioned to instantly respond to the commands of a general, even if the order seems to be unreasonable.

When God commanded Abraham to climb Mount Moriah and sacrifice his only son Isaac on the altar, that was the exact opposite of what Abraham felt like doing. God's command certainly didn't seem reasonable. But by faith Abraham obeyed because he believed God's promise that Isaac would be the father of a great nation was factual. He believed God would somehow bring Isaac back from the dead (Hebrews 11:19). After God provided a ram as a substitute sacrifice, Abraham descended the mountain with his beloved Isaac by his side. At that moment, Abraham was exuberant with joy based on facts, faith, and feelings.

When Christians fall to temptation, it's typically because they yield to temporary emotions and ignore the facts conveyed by Scripture. Why would a man have an affair with a woman at work when he has a beautiful wife and two kids at home? The response often goes something like, "Well, the electricity flowed between us and we couldn't stop the feelings so we just followed our hearts." Or, even worse, "I love my wife but I'm not 'in love' with her. Do you understand what I mean?" Frankly no, I don't understand.

Why would a woman who grew up in the church get sucked into a cult that is based on teaching that is contrary to the basics of Scripture? She rationalizes, "The teacher had such charisma. He was mesmerizing and it was really exciting to hear him speak. You could just sense that he had a special walk with the Lord." Why would a middle-aged couple on the verge of bankruptcy buy a new motorcycle? They later shake their heads in disbelief and try to explain, "We got so excited about it. The test-ride made us feel so young and free we just had to have it."

Satan's most lethal temptations leverage emotional appeals as opposed to intellectual doubts. Facts, faith and feelings…that's still the wise progression to follow for those who would walk in obedience to Christ. You may be accused of being hard-hearted and insensitive at times, but Jesus said, "If you love me, keep my commandments" (John 14:15).

I like the way *THE MESSAGE* paraphrases 1 Peter 1:14: "Don't lazily slip back into the old grooves of evil – just doing what you feel like doing. You didn't know any better then; you do now." Ephesians 4:13-15 in *The Living Bible* encourages us to "become full-grown in the Lord—yes, to the point of being filled full with Christ. Then we will no longer be like children, forever changing our minds about what we believe because someone has told us something different or has cleverly lied to us and made the lie sound like the truth. Instead, we will lovingly follow the truth at all times—speaking truly, dealing truly, living truly—and so become more and more in every way like Christ who is the Head of his body, the Church."

II. WE ARE TRANSFORMED MORALLY – we grow from yielding to our carnal desires to conforming to Christ's character.

First Peter 1:15-16 reads, "But just as he who called you is holy, so be holy in all you do; for it is written: 'Be holy, because I am holy.'" We usually think of holiness in negative terms, by focusing on what we shouldn't do. A holy person doesn't get drunk, doesn't do drugs, doesn't use profanity, doesn't commit adultery, doesn't lie, doesn't smoke, and doesn't cheat. But that doesn't capture the essence of the term. The word holy actually means "distinctive," "pure," "sacred," and "belonging to God."

Removing sinful activities is, of course, an aspect of holiness. The Bible says, "But among you there must not be even a hint of sexual immorality, or of any kind of impurity, or of greed, because these are improper for God's holy people" (Ephesians 5:3). So a part of holiness is keeping ourselves from immoral habits, profane speech and immodest appearance. But holiness is also more. Holiness is imitating God's character because we are God's children. Holiness is not just an appropriate amount of sin avoidance, but also a passionate pursuit of God's virtues—God is generous, God is impartial, God is faithful, God is merciful, God is love, God is humble, God is pure.

Authentic holiness is powerfully attractive. It is a moral courage, sacrificial love, and sheer joy that makes people sit up and say, "Wow! So that's what being a follower of Christ can look like!" It's being like Jesus, whose goodness drew people to Himself like a magnet. In a sentence, holiness is a life that looks like the one God would live if he walked in your shoes every day, having your job, your spouse, your kids, your friends, and your trials.

Holiness is not instantaneous, though. It's something you must develop as you grow in Christ. Simon Peter wrote, "For this very reason, make every effort to add to your faith goodness; and to goodness, knowledge; and to knowledge, self-control; and to self-control, perseverance; and to perseverance, godliness, and to godliness, mutual affection; and to mutual affection, love. *For if you possess these qualities in increasing measure*, they will keep you from being ineffective and unproductive in your knowledge of our Lord Jesus Christ" (2 Peter 1:5-8; emphasis added). Paul Rees said the Christian life is a gift and a growth. The gift of salvation is instantly given, but the growth into holiness is a process that takes time.

If you have a worldly background, you probably brought some profane habits into your new life in Christ and it may take a while to remove and replace them with God's holiness. It takes time to gradually change from conforming to our own evil desires to conforming to God's character. When a one-year old who is just learning to walk stumbles and falls, we giggle and encourage him to get back up. There's no harm done. But if a ten-year old repeatedly stumbles and falls, it's a sign of a serious problem. "As He called you is holy, so be holy in all you do."

Beginning with verse 16, Simon Peter gives four motivations for holiness, the first being a desire to resemble the heavenly Father. He writes "Be holy, because I am holy" (1 Peter 1:16). Paul conveys the same idea with, "Be imitators of God, therefore, as dearly loved children" (Ephesians 5:1). The older a boy becomes, the more he tends to look like and act like his father. The more you mature in the Christian life, the more you should resemble your heavenly Father.

The second motivator for holiness, a reverent fear of judgement, is conveyed in verse 17: "Since you call on a Father who judges each man's work impartially, live your lives as strangers here in reverent fear." The Bible says, "we must all appear before the judgment seat of Christ, so that each of us may receive what is due us for the things done while in the body, whether good or bad" (2 Corinthians 5:10). That's sobering! That's downright frightening! I don't want to have to face God and admit to defiant behavior or gross disobedience.

If you know there is a surveillance camera focused on you and recording your every move, you're very likely to behave. But that is precisely what God warns about when he declares that we will all have to give an account of every idle word and every deed done, even those done in secret (see Ecclesiastes 12:14 and Matthew 12:36). That is a powerful motivation to pursue holiness. Sometimes we do the right thing out of love for God. Sometimes we do the right things for fear of judgment.

A third motivation to pursue holiness is a recognition of the futility of unholy living. "For you know that it was not with perishable things such as silver or gold that you were redeemed from *the empty way of life* handed down to you from your forefathers" (1 Peter 1:18; emphasis added). Notice that Peter calls the ungodly life an empty life. How might you feel if you started the day with a hangover, or you got a good grade you didn't earn, or you woke up beside a person who doesn't share your name, your ring, or your future? You would feel extremely hollow, unfulfilled, guilty, and empty. And these are unfortunately common feelings. How many times do you have to experience that empty feeling before you conclude it's not worth it? What has to happen before you realize that the cost of sin is way out of proportion to its pleasure and decide that you're not going to buy it anymore?

The fourth motivator is the loving sacrifice of Jesus. 1 Peter 1:19-21 reads, "You were redeemed...with the precious blood of Christ, a lamb without blemish or defect. He was chosen before the creation of the world, but was revealed in these last times for your sake. Through him you believe in God, who raised him from the dead and glorified him, and so your faith and hope are in God." The cross was not an accident, it was an appointment. It was not a human tragedy, it was divine strategy. It was a part of God's plan before time began. Jesus Christ denied His personal desires and willingly sacrificed Himself on the cross for us because He loved us. It's not too much to ask for us to sacrifice some personal pleasure for Him.

Our church put on a powerful Easter Pageant every year for a decade. It told the life story of Jesus from His birth but about forty-five minutes was focused on His unjust arrest, trial, and crucifixion. It was so graphic and realistic that you could hear a pin drop when Jesus was being nailed to the cross. One night, an hour after the pageant was over, two young women sat solemnly on a couch in the lobby. They were obviously deeply convicted and troubled. A spiritual counselor approached them and asked, "Is there some way I can help you?" Choking back tears, they confessed that they had been living in a lesbian relationship, and knew they needed to repent and start living for Jesus. Not a word of the drama had been focused on immoral behavior. But just the visual of a loving Christ willingly dying on the cross for the sins of all people created in them a desire to be holy as He is holy.

Gratitude is a powerful motivator to pursue holiness. Only Jesus loved you enough to pour out His life-blood on your behalf. "Since He who called you is holy, be holy in all you do."

III. WE ARE TRANSFORMED RELATIONALLY –
we grow from being self-centered to being others-centered.

"Now that you have purified yourselves by obeying the truth so that you have sincere love for your brothers, love one another deeply, from the heart" (1 Peter 1:22). One of the most difficult lessons for children to learn is to be unselfish because they think the world revolves around them. That is not surprising given that the third word a child usually learns, after "mama" and "dada," is "mine." They have to be taught to go counter to their nature and share. The same is true for us. One of the most difficult lessons of the Christian life is to put others ahead of self. I want my needs met, my music sung, my kind of sermon preached, my seat reserved, my time respected, my child honored. If we don't get our way, we throw an adult temper tantrum.

In his book *The Life You've Always Wanted*, John Ortberg tells about a cranky old Christian named Hank who complained about everything for years. There came a period when his primary complaint was that the music in the church was too loud and Hank protested to the staff, the deacons, the ushers, and eventually even visitors. Some leaders finally told him that it was inappropriate to complain to strangers and he should limit his gripes to intimate friends. They thought that was the end of the saga but Ortberg goes on to recount, "A few weeks later, a secretary buzzed me on the intercom to say that an agent from OSHA…was here to see me." Hank had actually called the Occupational Safety and Health Administration and said, "The music at my church is too loud" so they sent a federal agent to check it out. "We don't mean to make light of this," Ortberg told him, "But nothing like this has ever happened before." "Don't apologize," the agent said. "Do you have any idea how much ridicule I've faced around my office since everyone discovered I was going out to bust a church?"

Hank had been in church for years but he had not grown beyond his own selfish interests. He'd wound visitors and the church's reputation. He'd throw a temper tantrum if he didn't get his way. Ortberg wrote, "Hank could not effectively love his wife or his children or people outside his family. He was easily irritated. He had little use for the poor and a casual contempt for those whose accents or skin pigment differed from his own. Whatever capacity he once might have had for joy or wonder or gratitude atrophied. He critiqued and judged and complained, and his soul got a little smaller each year."[1]

If we are deepening in our Christian walk, we move from being self-centered to others-centered. The Apostle Paul conveyed this principle with the appeal, "Do nothing out of selfish ambition or vain conceit, but in humility consider others better than yourselves. Each of you should look not only to your own interests, but also to the interests of others" (Philippians 2:3, 4). Warren Wiersbe shares the quote, "We share brotherly love because we are brothers and sisters in Christ and have likenesses. We share agape love because we belong to God and therefore can overlook differences."[2] It's a spiritual love, a sincere love, a sacrificial love.

Ed Swartz, a beloved father of four and a wonderful greeter in our church, took ill suddenly several years ago while attending a national Rotary Club meeting in Japan. When he began having serious symptoms, his wife Martha managed to get him to a Japanese hospital but she called home in total frustration because she was having trouble communicating. She had been with Ed in the hospital for a couple of days and was in serious need of a shower and translation assistance. We found the name of a Christian missionary in the vicinity and called her on Martha's behalf. Her name was Leone Cole and we discovered she was 89 years old, but very alert. She immediately said, "I'll take care of her." She took a train to the hospital, found Martha, brought her to her apartment, and allowed her to spend the night. She went back to the hospital with Martha and when Ed died, she ministered to her and kept her in her home until family members arrived days later. They were so grateful for this Christian servant who was an angel of mercy. The reason Leone cared was because of a common commitment to Jesus Christ.

When you became a Christian, you joined a network of Christian brothers and sisters all around the world who have learned to love one another deeply. It's called the Church. You are all bought with the same blood. You experienced the same new birth. You belong to the same Father. You enjoy the same spiritual nourishment. And that love deepens as you mature. You also take advantage of the opportunity to express love because you recognize

1. John Ortberg, *The Life You've Always Wanted* (Grand Rapids, MI: Zondervan), pp. 28, 29.
2. Warren Wiersbe, *The Wiersbe Bible study series: 1 Peter: How to make the best of times out of your worst of times* (Colorado Springs: David C. Cook, . 2011), p. 44.

that life is fleeting; "All men are like grass, and all their glory is like the flowers of the field; the grass withers and the flowers fall, but the word of the Lord stands forever.' And this is the word that was preached to you" (1 Peter 1:24, 25).

I have a friend who is a widower and really misses his wife. He will say to me often, "Tell your wife you love her every day." I know what he's saying. There comes a time when it's over and the chance to communicate and demonstrate it is gone, so it is essential that we allow our love to deepen while we can. For that to happen, you must get rid of wrong attitudes that alienate you from people. You need to "…rid yourselves of all malice and all deceit, hypocrisy, envy, and slander of every kind" (1 Peter 2:1).

Dave Hagler works as an umpire in a recreational softball league in Boulder, Colorado. He was pulled over for speeding some time ago and tried to talk the officer out of giving him a ticket. But the policeman was firm and, handing Dave the ticket, he curtly said, "If you don't like it, you can take it to court." Fast forward just a few weeks to when the softball season started. Dave was umpiring behind the plate and the first batter up to the plate was the police officer who had given him the ticket. It was an awkward moment when they recognized each other. The policeman stepped into the batter's box and asked, "How'd everything go with that ticket?" Without missing a beat, Hagler said, 'You better swing at everything!"

The worldly man harbors malice and seeks to get even. The mature Christian loves enough to forgive and forget. If you've been a Christian for a couple of decades but you're still nurturing hatred and bitterness, it's time to let it go. If you are still refusing to speak to people or still slandering people, it's time to grow up. You're being childish. Your growth has been stunted. Stop harboring anger, envy, and resentment. Don't try to get even by deception and slander. Be mature and forgive those who have offended you. Don't go to your grave harboring a grudge. Rather "be transformed into His image."

The secret of deepening your love is to saturate yourself with the Word of God. Be filled with His truth. "Like newborn babies, crave pure spiritual milk, so that by it you may grow up in your salvation" (1 Peter 2:2). The Bible is compared to meat and milk, and bread and honey. It's food for your soul. It nourishes you and gives you the capacity to love beyond yourself. We used to sing, "Give me that old time religion… [it] makes me love everybody." When the love of Christ is in us, He gives us what we need to love beyond what we can do on our own.

I tried to think of a good example of someone who was transformed by Christ in all three of these areas we've discussed—mentally, morally and relationally. I came up with an excellent example—Simon Peter. When he first came to Christ he was driven by emotion. He was up and down, confessing Christ as Lord one minute and telling him he was wrong the next. But, over time, Simon Peter deepened and became a man of obedience and consistency, willing to give his own life in order to be faithful to Christ.

Simon Peter wasn't a very holy man when we first meet him in Scripture. He was somewhat egotistical, he demanded center stage, and was known to lose his cool and even curse on occasion. But when he grew to be like His heavenly Father, he insisted no one pay him homage, and he took abuse without retaliating.

When Peter first came to Christ, he wasn't very loving toward others. He was prejudiced toward people of other races and even tried to kill a man with his sword. But Peter deepened in love and sensitivity. He entered the home of a Gentile named Cornelius and shared the gospel with his family. He stopped at the sight of a blind beggar and said, 'We'd like to really help you."

Peter modeled what it means to prepare the mind for action and move from being emotionally driven to Scripturally-driven. He showed how to become like God in holiness and to move from conforming to his own selfish desires to imitating God's character. And he showed us how to love others deeply and be transformed from being self-centered to being others-centered. Simon Peter has earned the right to encourage us to be like newborn babies who crave spiritual milk, so that by it you may grow up in your salvation, "now that you have tasted that the Lord is good."

Application Questions

1. Do you find it most difficult to mature mentally, morally, or relationally? What factors in your life make growth in that area particularly difficult?

2. Since becoming a Christian, have you matured most mentally, morally, or relationally? What are the practical ways in which that growth has affected the ways you think, act, and interact?

3. What strategies do you currently employ to grow mentally, morally, and relationally? What strategies do you find most effective?

4. How do you use your influence as a church leader to encourage your congregation to achieve spiritual growth? How do you influence individual congregants to achieve spiritual growth?

5. Are your church's worship services, programs, and ministries primarily emotionally-driven or scripturally-driven? What would an appropriate balance between the two look like? What can you do as a church leader to strike that appropriate balance?

Group Discussion Questions

1. If you could perfectly reflect Jesus in one way, what would it be? How would that positively impact your attitudes, behaviors, and relationships?

2. What tools and resources does your church provide to help people experience spiritual growth? Which ones are most effective for you?

3. Which of the following is the most compelling motivation for you to pursue holiness? What makes it particularly persuasive?

    a. Desire to resemble God

    b. A reverent fear of judgement

    c. Futility of unholy living

    d. The loving sacrifice of Jesus

4. Why do you think so many Christians fail to achieve spiritual growth and, as a result, look very much the same as they did many years after accepting Christ? Who is responsible for the lack of growth? What are the solutions?

5. On a scale of 1 (not at all) to 10 (a lot), to what degree have you grown from being self-centered to others-centered since becoming a Christian? How has that growth impacted your attitudes, behaviors, and relationships?

the CALL
to TRANSFORMATION

TIM WALLINGFORD

CHAPTER 2

CHURCH

Jesus said, "…I will build my church, and the gates of Hades will not overcome it" (Matthew 16:18). The Greek term for church is *ekklesia*. It means "those called out to assemble; or ones separated or designated for a mission; or ones set apart." About 400 years before Christ, *Ekklesia* was associated with a soldier summoned to join the army for battle. By 200 B.C., it had become more general and *Ekklesia* represented a citizen of a Greek city. Each citizen was *called out* 30 to 40 times a year to carry on the town's business. By the time of Christ, the term was used for a chosen group of people serving Caesar. The *Ekklesia*, as well as governors, helped establish Roman authority across the empire. Caesar's *Ekklesia* was composed of military men, business men, teachers, and leaders in various fields.

They were *called out* to be trained in Roman language, laws, arts, and customs. Once they were thoroughly trained, the *Ekklesia* were *sent into* newly conquered territories to live amongst the barbarians integrating them into Roman society by teaching and modeling the Roman way. Once the *Ekklesia* were established in a new location, they were called a Roman colony. Philippi, Corinth, and Thessalonica were started by Caesar's *Ekklesia*. The strategic use of *Ekklesia* was a factor in Rome's longevity as a united Empire.

Understanding this background gives us insight into Jesus' definition of church, doesn't it? Jesus said he would call out of the world a group of people to be his very own, a distinct and holy people—his *Ekklesia*. With these called-out ones, Jesus would create a new race composed of all ethnicities to form an eternal kingdom. Jesus would train, empower, and live through each of his *Ekklesia* to fulfill his global mission. Matthew 10 is the first place Jesus used this technique. The twelve disciples were trained in the ways of Christ's kingdom then sent out to establish beachheads within the neighborhoods. They ministered to people and proclaimed the gospel.

This same strategy was used by the early church for the first several hundred years. *Oikos* (house) churches were established throughout the neighborhoods within the Roman Empire (Colossians 1:6). The members of each house church, or the *Ekklesia*, would go out into the neighborhoods as the "...light of the world...that they may see your good works and glorify your Father in Heaven" (Matthew 5:14-16). The early *Ekklesia* viewed themselves *going out* as Christ's army (Matthew 10: 34; 26:47; 2 Corinthians 10:3-5; Ephesians 6:1-10; 2 Timothy 3:3, 4). The mission involved training to conquer the hearts of the people with the gospel, proclaiming Jesus as the King of Kings.

It is this military viewpoint of the earliest called-out ones that gives us the word sacrament. The word is not found in Scripture but paints a picturesque view of the early church's identity. To enter Caesar's army, one had to take the sacramentum. The Latin word refers to a life-changing oath. The sacramentum was an elaborate ceremony where a man pledged his allegiance to Caesar. After taking the sacramentum, all his possessions, even his life belonged to Caesar to advance his interests. Anyone who was not in the Roman army was called a pagan (one who had not taken the oath).

Early Christians witnessed this ceremony and declared, "We too have a King, Jesus. We too take a life-changing oath in baptism. We pledge our lives, possessions, everything to the advancement of his kingdom." Each week, at the Lord's Supper these soldiers of Christ would sup with their King re-affirming their oaths to live and die for his mission. Christ's *Ekklesia* also categorized pagans (ordinary citizens) as civilians, meaning those who had not taken the life-changing oath. The *Ekklesia* believed they would convince the civilians to join Christ's army (Acts 26:28, 29).[3]

3. Joe Ellis, *The Church on Purpose: Keys to Effective Church Leadership* (Cincinnati, OH: Standard Publishing, 1982), p. 47-48.

JESUS STILL LIVES IN THE NEIGHBORHOOD

According to Scripture how does a person become a member of the *Ekklesia*? We give our "life-changing" oath in the Good Confession. "I believe that Jesus is the Christ, the son of the living God and my personal Lord and Savior" (Matthew 16:16). We then are baptized into Christ. Through this spiritual union, the individual is united to Christ becoming a part of his physical body. The *Ekklesia* is now Christ's hands, feet and voice going into neighborhoods with the life-changing gospel (Romans 6:3-11; 1 Corinthians 12:12).

John described Jesus' life and ministry this way, "The Word became flesh and blood and moved into the neighborhood" (John 1:14; The Message). So, where did Jesus live? Where did he work? In the neighborhood. He met the neighbors, learned their names, heard their needs, ate with them, and ministered to the individual people. Jesus was a friend to sinners (Matthew 11:19). He went into Peter's house and healed his mother-in-law (Matthew 8:14). Jesus had dinner at Levi's house and met tax collectors and sinners (9:10). Jesus went into the leader of the synagogue's home and raised his daughter from the dead (Matthew 9:23).

Jesus went through all the towns getting to know the neighbors. He healed their individual sicknesses, then proclaimed the good news of his kingdom (Matthew 9:35). Living in the neighborhood, Jesus saw and heard the brokenness. They were like sheep without a shepherd. They were "harassed and helpless" (Matthew 9:36). The Greek words are revealing. *Harassed* carries the idea of flaying a fish. Life had sliced and diced the people's hearts, dreams, and families. The word for *helpless* shows a people defeated, lying prostrate on the ground with life's foot pressing their faces into the dirt. It was then when Jesus turned to his disciples proclaiming, "The harvest is plentiful but the workers are few. Ask the Lord of the harvest, therefore, to send out workers into his harvest field" (Matthew 9:37, 38).

Do you see what Jesus called *Ekklesia* work? It was to love our neighbors strategically to win them to Christ. Notice how Jesus defined the neighborhood? First, he called it *his* harvest field. Jesus owned the neighborhood. He had the right to dwell there. He was not afraid or repulsed by its condition. Again, he loved his neighborhood so much he willingly died to fix it (John 3:16). Second, it's his *harvest field*. The neighborhood was where his *Ekklesia* scattered the seed, cultivated the soil, watered the crops, pulled the weeds, and then harvested good fruit (see Matthew 13). Jesus called the neighborhood "ripe" (John 4:35). Ripe meant the fruit was ready to pick and if not harvested would rot.

In other words, people without Christ will pay for their sins in the eternal lake of fire, Hell (Matthew 3:10, 12; 7:19; 13:40, 42, 50; 22: 7; 25:41). The cross of Christ is for everyone. The question is, how will people hear this good news? Jesus' plan is to tell our neighbors through us. We are the body of Christ, his *Ekklesia*. We are the conduit of Christ. He speaks, loves, cares for them through us. We explain that God created them in their mothers' wombs (Psalm 139). He knows their names. We reveal what sin does to their relationships with God, others, and the personal damage it creates in each of them. We share the fact that God's love is greater, demonstrated by Jesus dying for their sins on the cross. God's greatest desire is to heal their brokenness by giving them new lives.

As we are working in our neighborhoods, we must examine the growth of our strategic interactions. We must watch, praying for our neighbors' hearts to open as God uses our cultivating efforts of love and truth telling. Then it will happen. Through careful monitoring, we will see our neighbors' hearts turn "ripe." So we then can ask the question, "Are you ready to accept Christ, repent, and be baptized" (Acts 2:38)? Once they believe, take the oath, then we baptize them into Christ. Christ then transplants them into his kingdom. The *Ekklesia* expands—the army of Christ grows.

COMING TO GRIPS WITH CHURCH

When you think of the word church, what image comes to mind? You probably automatically picture a building, a place, a worship service, an event, a program, or a minister, right? We often say, "I'm going to church." Or, "I'm in search of a church." Or, "I like or dislike that church." In our minds, "church" is a building with a street address where people gather for a worship service or other religious event. Even the Merriam-Webster online dictionary defines church as "a building for public and especially Christian worship."[4]

---

4. "Church," *Merriam Websters Online Dictionary.* https://www.merriam-webster.com/dictionary/ church. Accessed October, 2017.

It is not surprising then that when we talk about restoring, renewing, adding on, or renovating the church, our minds immediately think of a building. According to the *Wall Street Journal*, in 2015 over three billion dollars was spent erecting about 4,000 new church buildings. In 2013, research from the Evangelical Credit Union found, in churches surveyed, that about 75% of the offerings were spent on buildings, real estate, technology, the maintenance of those facilities and staff salaries.[5]

I have nothing against church buildings. Christians need a place to meet. My point is—as we have just learned from studying the New Testament Scriptures—when the word church is mentioned, no one thought of a building or a program. It always refers to believers in Christ who are the house, building, temple where the living Christ dwells. "O do you not know that your body is the temple of the Holy Spirit within you, whom you have from God..." (1 Corinthians 6:19; ESV).

According to the New Testament, renovating the church meant transforming believers into the character and mission of Christ. It's the life-long process the Bible calls sanctification. It's a common theme throughout the New Testament. It begins the moment a person exits the baptistery. The apostle Paul wrote, "Do not conform to the pattern of this world, but be transformed by the renewing of your mind..." (Romans 12:2).

DO I GO TO CHURCH? NO, I *AM* THE CHURCH

There are two basic disciple-making approaches today: Corporate and personal evangelism. I've used both. Corporate evangelism means that the Sunday morning worship service is shaped to bring the neighbors to church. Corporate evangelism utilizes the attractional model of evangelism. Church can be defined as a place, event, program, or experience. We start with the neighborhood profile then shape the service, the setting, the music, the videos, and the message to attract or appeal to the neighborhood around us. We go to church. Our goal is to attract our neighbors to the Sunday event. There are congregations that do seeker-driven or seeker-sensitive services well, with a defined, effective discipleship process that turns the lost into Christ-like followers. However, many attractional churches are failing to

5. Tom Shultz, "The Shocking Truth of Church Budgets." https://holysoup.com/the-shocking-truth-of-church-budgets. Accessed November, 2017.

turn the neighborhood consumer into the committed Christian.

This approach of defining the church as a building, a program, or an evangelistic event has had a devastating effect on American Christians. It's difficult to preach the whole counsel of God if our goal is to not offend or drive visitors away. George Barna laments, "Every day the church is becoming more like the world it allegedly seeks to change"[6]

As we've already seen, New Testament evangelism was very different. It involved training believers to be the church; Christ's *Ekklesia*. Then the *Ekklesia* obediently fulfilled the Great Commission (Matthew 28:19, 20) by going into their neighborhoods as the living, physical body of Christ. The "wow" should not be the Sunday morning "show." The "wow" is the miracle of the believers' changed lives. A changed life validates salvation, gives Christ-like character and confirms the gospel message as authentic. Sunday mornings we gather to sup with our living Lord. We renew our oaths to be his *Ekklesia*. We declare with one voice, "Worthy is the Lamb, who was slain, to receive power and wealth and wisdom and strength and honor and glory and praise" (Revelation 5:12)! Then we are exhorted and equipped to take on the character and mission of our King (Ephesians 4:11-16). Evangelism is done as we, the *Ekklesia*, scatter throughout our neighborhoods Monday through Saturday.

CHURCH: THE FIRST 300 YEARS

Consider first the Church's beginning. Christianity was an illegal religion for most of the first three hundred years of its existence. Romans believed Caesar was god. They participated daily in emperor worship which involved burning incense in public squares and at their workplaces. Christians, of course, refused to worship Caesar as god. The Romans began to believe the Christians were members of a secret kingdom which would rise and attempt to overthrow the Empire.

So, the Caesars persecuted the followers of Christ. There were ten major persecutions. Christians were not permitted to own property. They could lose their jobs, be put on racks, be burned at the stake, or be thrown to lions.

---

6. Ronald Sider, "The Scandal of the Evangelical Conscience: Why Don't Christians Live what They Preach?" *Christianity Today*, Feb. 2005. http://www.booksandculture.com/articles/2005/janfeb/3.8.html. Accessed October 2017.

The *Ekklesia* met in homes (Romans 16:5), a Christian-owned business or hall (Acts 19:9), and even in the catacombs. That's right; worship services were literally held underground, in caves, throughout the second and third centuries. Christians gathered to worship the living Christ amongst the buried bodies of many martyred for the faith. Worship services were held in secret, in hiding, for fear of execution. Non-believers were prohibited from participating in worship for fear they were spies who would report the church's location to authorities.

Around A.D. 260, Emperor Valerian ended the persecution of Christians. His son, Gallienus ordered properties returned to Christians. Many wealthy believers donated their larger homes to be used as meeting places. For the next forty years Christians were able to purchase property, usually adjacent to their cemeteries, allowing them to expand their houses of prayer to accommodate larger gatherings. In A.D. 303, this explosion of church buildings irked the reigning Caesar, Diocletian. As he sat watching the church buildings being constructed through his window, he was convicted that Christianity was destroying Roman values. He then launched one of the most brutal persecutions to date that involved the destruction of all houses of prayer. Christians were once again forced to worship in homes and underground cemeteries.

In spite of this persecution, conservative estimates are that the church grew by 40% annually.[7] How did this happen? The early Church defined their identity as the *Ekklesia* of Christ considering it an honor to suffer for their living king. They were called to obedience, to take on Christ's character and mission. Neighbors could see the believers' resilient faith, their love for each other, the way they forgave others, prayed for their enemies, and their willingness to die for Jesus. It was the Christians' love and holiness that was striking. The neighborhood knew Christ was real and that the gospel message would bring forgiveness and transformation to them as well. Around A.D. 150, Justin Martyr wrote to Emperor Pius to explain that Christians were not a threat to the Empire. Notice his emphasis on the lifestyle of believers.

"Formerly we rejoiced in uncleanness of life. Now we only rejoice in chastity. Before we used magic arts. Now we dedicate ourselves to the true

---

7. Rodney Stark, *Rise of Christianity: A Sociologist Reconsiders History.* (Princeton, NJ: Princeton University Press), p. 161.

God. Before we loved money and possessions more than anything. Now we share what we have, to everyone in need. Before we hated and killed one another and would not eat with those of another race. But now since the manifestation of Christ, we have come to a common life and pray for our enemies to *win over* those who hate us without just cause" (emphasis added).[8]

CONSTANTINE'S CHURCH

The Emperor Constantine's conversion from paganism to Christianity ushered in the use of church buildings. Christianity was declared legal for the first time in 300 years. Property was restored to the Jesus followers. Constantine began to tear down pagan temples erecting basilicas in their places. The Romans often called the public building, housing a god. The Latin word for basilica means the place where the king reigns. Constantine, with his background in paganism, believed the god he worshipped lived in a physical temple. Once he became a worshipper of Christ, he felt Jesus needed a place in which to dwell and reign so basilicas were built. Every location connected to the life of Christ—his birth, temptation, Sermon on the Mount, key miracles, crucifixion, and resurrection—all had a basilica. And because Christ is the King of Kings, his basilicas were the tallest and most elaborately designed buildings around. The neighborhood was then expected to go to worship in a church building, where Jesus lived.

Constantine's version of church had massive crowds converting to Christianity by simply attending church and making the good confession. Gone was the catechumen, a lengthy training course that included several years of instruction for interested believers who wanted baptism. Years later Augustine rebuked the church for getting away from the catechumen. Augustine believed that this was the reason Christians had begun to live such carnal lifestyles. Without receiving biblical instruction prior to baptism and continued teaching with accountability after baptism, they didn't know they needed to transform into the character and mission of Christ.[9]

---

8. Justin Martyr, *The First Apology*. http://www.newadvent.org/fathers/0126.htm. Accessed October, 2017.
9. Arnold Clinton, "Early Church Catechesis and New Christians' Classes in Contemporary Evangelism." http://www.etsjets.org/files/JETS-PDFs/47/47-1/47-1-pp039-054_JETS.pdf. Accessed October, 2017.

AMERICAN CHURCH

In 1790, Samuel Slater, who is known as the Father of the American Industrial Revolution, opened his cotton mill in Rhode Island. Interestingly enough, another idea that Slater brought from England was Sunday school. Slater would hire teenagers to work in the mill, but also to attend classes that included reading, writing, arithmetic, and the Scriptures.[10]

The Industrial Age brought mass production to America, which gave rise to the Middle Class. Common people began dressing up to attend social events of every kind to demonstrate their newly improved financial and social statuses. The conservative denominations condemned this emphasis on elaborate clothing and bigger and better homes as worldly. Preachers like John Wesley and Charles Finney believed it was a barrier to unity. They even went so far as to prohibit individuals from attending Methodist classes if they wore anything elegant.

The Episcopal, Congregational, and Unitarian churches took a different approach. Preachers like Horace Bushnell from Connecticut argued that "…sophistication and refinement were attributes of God." This theological perspective stressed that Christians should dress elegantly to honor God. This emphasis on the exterior led many poor people to buy a suit to wear on Sunday, just to sell it on Monday to pay for the groceries that week.[11]

At this time, churches also began constructing elaborate church buildings. They began adding choirs and organs to their worship services. People began to leave the plain, more conservative Methodist and Baptist churches for the fancier worship services and buildings. Concerned that their members were joining other congregations, many conservative churches began upgrading their buildings and worship services as well. With that, the attractional church service method had hit America. It's also interesting that John Wesley's concerns proved right. Middle-class America tended to levitate to the Episcopal, Congregational and Unitarian congregations, while the poorer American was "attracted" to the worship service that reflected his or her social class.[12]

---

10. "Samuel Slater" Wikipedia. https://en.wikipedia.org/wiki/Samuel_Slater. Accessed October, 2017.
11. Truth According to Scripture. "The Origin of Dressing Up for Church." http://www.truthaccordingtoscripture.com/documents/church-practice/dressing-up/dressing-up-for-church.php#.WfObB1RSxdg. Accessed October, 2017.
12. Ibid.

A NEW MISSION STATEMENT

There's nothing wrong in and of itself with a church building, but while Jesus was on earth, his evangelistic strategy was never to erect a building or to expect broken and spiritually blind people who did not know their right from their left (Jonah 4:11) to know enough to come to church to find salvation. Jesus walked over 3,000 miles in 3 ½ years "…to seek and save the lost" (Luke 19:10). Study the parables. Doesn't the good shepherd leave the ninety-nine to go search for the one that is lost? Then, when the shepherd brings the restored one into the gathering, isn't there's a great celebration (Luke 15:3-7)? Doesn't the woman who has ten coins but loses one, sweep and search all night until she finds the one that was lost (Luke 15: 8-10)?

That's why Jesus "went into all the towns and villages…" (Matthew 9:35). Going into the neighborhood was THE strategy Jesus taught his disciples (Matthew 10:7; Luke 10:1). "…you will be my witnesses in Jerusalem, Judea, Samaria and to the ends of the earth" (Acts 1:8). Apart from the miraculous outpouring of the Holy Spirit on the apostles at Pentecost (Acts 2), going into the neighborhoods is the ONLY church strategy we see in the book of Acts.

Scripture says it's up to every Christian to clarify the true gospel, laying out for our families, friends, and neighbors the conditions God requires for them to receive salvation. God also promises power to make us bold in persuading others (2 Corinthians 3:12). The Greek word for *bold is* "to go public." It carries the idea of being free, open to share in public. The apostle Paul said God commissions us to go public with the gospel. So, "…who is up to the task" (2 Corinthians 2:16)? Paul said we are. It is God who makes us competent for this ministry of reconciliation (2 Corinthians 3:6).

But how does God make us competent to be his *Ekklesia*? Is there a training manual God has written for us to study that teaches us how to reach our neighborhoods for Christ? Can we truly identify the barriers that keep our neighbors from salvation? Absolutely! It starts with every Christian adopting a new mission statement for their lives. It should read something like this: ***Be like Jesus in character and mission.*** Our writers are praying God will use this book to enable you to live out your mission in everyday life. This is your call, your purpose in life; the very reason God has re-created you (Ephesians 2:10).

This book's primary focus is becoming like Jesus in character. To be an *Ekklesia* for Christ, *we must be transformed.* It is this miracle of changed lives that makes our witness credible and our message authentic. We must daily die to self, allowing Christ to transform us into his image, the image we lost to sin. We have no witness and we cannot be the light of the world if we are not being changed into the image of God (2 Corinthians 5:17; Ephesians 5:1). *So, this book's entire purpose is dedicated to who, what, where, when, and why of spiritual transformation.*

Application Questions

1. What implications does Matthew 16:18 hold for your church and for you personally as a church leader?

2. How do you personally get out into the neighborhood to meet unbelievers, learn their names, meet their needs, dine with them, and minister to them?

3. Do you personally lean more naturally toward corporate evangelism or personal evangelism? How is your preference reflected in your church's messages, worship services, and programs, and ministries?

4. How would you carry out your role as a church leader if there weren't any church buildings, or if those buildings were no longer a viable meeting place?

5. What is your personal mission statement? How does it impact the way you engage your neighborhood?

Group Discussion Questions

1. What are some specific ways Christians should reflect the fact that they are "called out" by Christ? How do those characteristics make you more relevant, credible, and engaging to your neighborhood?

2. In what ways has churches changed since Christians began gathering for corporate worship in large buildings instead of homes? In what ways, and to what degree, have the changes been productive and unproductive?

3. Why was the early Church able to experience growth in spite of severe persecution? Does the Church experience more or less growth during periods of persecution?

4. Why is showing love to your neighbors important in an effort to win them to Christ? What are some of the most effective ways that you can show love to your neighbors?

5. In what ways can it be tricky for Christians to be bold in their faith while at the same time showing love to their neighbors? How can Christians overcome those challenges?

CHAPTER 3

CHURCH TRANSFORMATION

OUR FALL

When it came to the creation of man, God stated, "Let us make mankind in our image, in our likeness…" (Genesis 1:26). The Hebrew words for "image" and "likeness" are used elsewhere in the Bible to refer to "concrete statues that portray the exact representation of the god."[13]

God the Father verbalized to God the Holy Spirit a clear blueprint for mankind. Humans were to have a personality with the ability to reason, make moral decisions, be creative, strategize, exercise free will, and self-control; qualities necessary to have fellowship with God. Genesis 3:8 shows the realization of his plan; God walked, talked, interacted, listened and responded to Adam and Eve in the garden.

Genesis 1:28 states a second purpose for mankind bearing God's image: man is to be THE representation of the one true God. God delegated to Adam dominion and managerial authority of the world. A beautiful picture of this partnership is when God brought to Adam every genus of animal that God had created, allowing Adam to name them. With God standing by his side, Adam completed his assignment (Genesis 2:20). What an awesome privilege. God created man to have dominion over his world, while remaining accountable to the ultimate King, the Creator God.

---

13. Paul Kissling, *The College Press NIV Commentary Genesis VOLUME 1* (Joplin, MO: College Press Publishing, 2004), p. 124.

The responsibility to manage creation, though, came with free will. When he gave mankind free will, God placed the future of the world in the hands of man. The awesome privilege brought breathtaking *responsibility*. At any time, Adam and Eve could choose to reject God's authority. That was the purpose of the "…tree of the knowledge of good and evil…" (Genesis 2:17). If at any point Adam and Eve chose to reject God's sovereignty, they could eat of that tree. God also communicated the consequences to them, "…you will surely die" (Genesis 2:17). The Hebrew word means, "to be separated from, or bring to an end."[14] God explained to Adam that this act of disobedience would destroy their relationship. Rebellion toward God meant loss of their position as managerial leaders of the world.

Shortly after the inauguration of the partnership, Satan tricked Adam and Eve by depicting God as a deceiver. Satan's narrative: God has lied to you therefore, he cannot be trusted. The Serpent argued that God was threatened by the possibility that they too could reach divine status if they ate from the tree. Deceived, Adam and Eve wanted the throne, they wanted rule of the world – in short, they wanted to become like God. The consequences of that first sin were separation from God, the introduction of death, frustration and tension within creation, increased pain in childbearing, disease, guilt, shame, and imperfect relationships marred by manipulation, deception, and bondage (Genesis 3). Genesis 3-6 and other Scriptures demonstrate that the fall resulted in the human heart becoming diseased, wicked, and a lawbreaker with a tendency to rebel (Genesis 6:5-8; Jeremiah 17:9).

Adam and Eve failed as God's stewards and fell under the bondage of another master, Satan, who ruled the hearts of humankind (John 12:31, 14:30). As absolute ruler, God could have asserted his kingship by destroying mankind. The flood came close but, by God's grace, Noah and his family were spared. In God's great mercy, he created a plan to remove sin and its resulting brokenness, to transform the broken world back to his original design. Humans will be able to have relationships with their Creator, and be restored to their rightful places as managers of God's world. But this plan would not violate his righteous character, holy principles, or sovereignty. God cannot and will not capitulate to Satan.

---

14. Colin Brown, ed., *The New International Dictionary of New Testament Theology* (Grand Rapids, MI: Zondervan, 1975).

The plan was publicly announced in Genesis 3:15. With a broad stroke, God painted a picture of the eventual arrival of someone who will be born of woman and who will crush the head of the serpent. Jesus will remove the bondage and power of Satan through the cross and resurrection. Through the Messiah, God will transform all things back to their original state.

IT STARTS WITH DISCIPLESHIP

The term "disciple" appears 261 times in the New Testament. The term "Christian" is found only three times (Acts 11:26; 26:28; 1 Peter 4:16). Disciple means "one taught." The Greek word is *mathetes.* It identified a pupil, an apprentice, or a follower of a certain teacher. John the Baptist had disciples. The Pharisees identified themselves as disciples of Moses. Peter, Andrew, James, and the rest of the twelve became students and apprentices of Jesus. A disciple of Christ is one who takes on the character and mission of Christ by learning Jesus' teachings and by imitating his lifestyle. The goal is to learn the facts, add up the information, and apply them properly. We add Christ to our life and multiply Christ through others.

Matthew 28:19, 20 are the last recorded words of Jesus. Christians call this the Great Commission:

> Therefore, go and make *disciples* of all nations, baptizing them in the name of the Father and of the Son and of the Holy Spirit, and *teaching* them to obey *everything* I have commanded you. And surely I am with you always, to the very end of the age (emphasis added).

Jesus is not calling a person to *make a "decision" for Christ*, but to *be made into his "disciple."* That's an enormous difference! How does this work?

First, the Great Commission starts by explaining that the gospel brings both forgiveness and transformation. Before baptism, a person should understand that forgiveness of sins and discipleship are two parts of the salvation package. Some teach that salvation and discipleship are separate issues, but to be baptized means you are committing your life to be Christ's follower.

Second, being a disciple means learning "to obey everything [Christ]... commanded" (Matthew 28:20). Jesus said, "the student is not above the teacher, but everyone who is *fully trained* will be like their teacher" (Luke 6:40; emphasis added). Jesus then challenges his disciples to recognize the "...log that is in your own eyes..." (v. 41). With the goal to become like Jesus, the disciple immediately begins the work of identifying sins and habits that must be replaced with holy behavior. To be *fully trained* is the disciple's goal. The Greek word is *katartizo* meaning to be completely and thoroughly mended, re-made, and restored to the original. The process includes solid Bible teaching and becoming an apprentice of a mature believer who models Christ's character and mission.

The Greek word for "teaching" (Matthew 28: 19), is a present-active participle, meaning that the idea is to "continually instruct." If we take the same Greek word and express it as a noun, the word "teaching" takes on the meaning of "master instructor, scholar." Jesus is saying that disciple-making involves much more than getting people to give the good confession. Christ's apprentices should eventually become master teachers. This applies to every believer. When the writer of Hebrews rebuked the Jewish believers for being "...dull of hearing..." he stated, "For though by this time you ought to be teachers, you need someone to teach you again the basic principles..." (Hebrews 5:12; ESV). The writer reprimanded those believers for having the wrong goal. Instead of agonizing over their problems, Christ called them to strive to become *master instructors* of God's word.

Jesus had perfect integrity. His teaching and lifestyle were one-hundred percent aligned. That is our goal. Though it will not be totally actualized until we receive our new resurrected bodies, it is every disciple's goal to be *fully trained*—re-made, mended, restored to God's image. Learning Christ's commands and imitating his lifestyle with the help of godly mentors is the formula the Holy Spirit uses to transform disciples into Christ-like character and then to live out Christ's mission in their neighborhoods.

Finally, the candidate for salvation and discipleship must count the cost of being forgiven and transformed. In Luke 14:7-24, Jesus described Heaven as a wedding banquet that affords endless joy, provisions, laughter, and fellowship.

Jesus' next comment was shocking, though. He turned to the crowd and basically stated, "But it will cost you everything" (Luke 14:25-35).

SALVATION COSTS EVERYTHING

The Bible presents many implications of God's redemption plan. One that is often forgotten is that salvation has a cost:

1. We must love Jesus more than our families and our own lives (Luke 14:25, 26). Our love for Christ must be so radical and extraordinary that our devotion to self and family in comparison will look like hate.

2. We must be willing to take up our crosses and follow him (Luke 14:27). Death on a cross is slow and torturous. It is the process of discipleship that involves daily dying to selfish desires, putting on Christ's character, and doing his mission. It is the willingness to bear reproach and loss for the name of Jesus.

3. We must renounce all that we have to be Christ's disciples (Luke 14:33). "So therefore, any one of you who does not renounce all that he has cannot be my disciple." "No servant can serve two masters, for either he will hate the one and love the other, or he will be devoted to the one and despise the other. You cannot serve God and money" (Luke 16:13). Jesus was speaking of the two lords—God or money. We can't add Jesus to a life of self-centeredness, personal goals, and accomplishments to round out our materialistic life. We can't add on to our present lifestyles and schedules a new religious compartment.

4. We must count the cost before we decide (Luke 14:28-32). Jesus expects us to finish. He wants to complete our transformation then glorify us at his second coming. To press his point Jesus used examples; doesn't a builder count the cost before he begins to build a tower? Doesn't an army general do a thorough evaluation before entering a war? He was telling us we must count the cost before we decide to be disciples of Christ.

Jesus concluded with an illustration using salt. We know that if salt is exposed to moisture the chlorine and sodium can dissolve leaving a crystal that looks like salt but with no salty effects. It's useless. Jesus' point is that finishing is better than starting. To become his disciple but then to not finish for any reason would be like salt that has lost its saltiness. It's worthless and will be tossed into the manure pile (14:34). The implication is alarming. To be called as a disciple but to be without transformation is failure to fulfill the purpose. This is useless to God and the individual will be thrown into the eternal lake of fire (Luke 14:35).

The word Christian is a wonderful title for believers, even though the contexts of the three times it is used in the New Testament (Acts 11:26; 26:28; I Peter 4:16) could suggest it was a label created by pagans. For example, King Agrippa sarcastically asked Paul, "Do you think that in such a short time you can persuade me to be a Christian" (Acts 26:28)? Peter used the title to identify with the reproach and suffering of Christ (1 Peter 4:16). At Antioch, Luke stated that believers were first *called* Christians at Antioch (Acts 11:26).

There's evidence to suggest the title mocked Christ's followers as arrogant people who thought of themselves as morally better than everyone else.[15] The apostle Peter referred to this irony when he wrote, "With respect to this they are surprised when you do not join them in the same flood of debauchery, and they malign you" (1 Peter 4:4; ESV).

The title Christian conveys a relationship to Christ. We belong to Christ. We are of his household. We are his servants (1 Corinthians 3:9), called to carry out our duties. We are to serve our Master well. Our goal is to hear from Jesus, "Well done, good and faithful servant..." (Matthew 25:21; ESV). To be a faithful servant, we must be "fully trained" (Luke 6:40; ESV).

Discipleship is about being transformed into Christ's character and Christ's mission (2 Corinthians 3:18).

---

15. "What Does the Name Christian Mean?" ichthys.com/mail-the-name-Christian.htm. Accessed October, 2017.

We Are Christ's Letter of Recommendation

THE BACKGROUND

Paul's authenticity as an apostle is established in 2 Corinthians. False teachers had infiltrated the church at Corinth. They probably had Jewish backgrounds and they insisted that to be saved Christ followers must incorporate elements of the Old Testament law into their Christianity. This probably included Jewish circumcision and the Sabbath rituals.

It was common in New Testament times for teachers to carry with them letters of recommendation. The New Testament had not been completed at the time (A.D. 53), so Christ's disciples had no canon by which to judge an unknown preacher's doctrine. Letters of recommendation from Jerusalem would squelch any suspicion of a visiting speaker misrepresenting the gospel. Without modern communication methods, it was virtually impossible to get immediate verification on a teacher's credentials from the church in Jerusalem which often was some distance away. The church began in Jerusalem. The so called "pillars" of the faith; the apostles Peter, James and John lived there (Galatians 2:9). This is why letters from the church in Jerusalem carried so much authority.

The false teachers at Corinth had been able to gain status in the church at Corinth through letters of recommendation from the church leaders in Jerusalem. Probably the letters had not come from the apostles but from Pharisees who had converted to Christianity. To discredit the apostle Paul, they had convinced Corinthian believers that Paul's doctrine had not been endorsed by the church in Jerusalem. They were asking, "Where is Paul's letter of recommendation?"

Paul's letters of recommendation were the transformed lives of the believers at Corinth:

> You yourselves are our *letter of recommendation* written on our hearts, to be known and read by all. You show that you are a letter from Christ delivered by us, written not with ink but with the Spirit of the living God, not on tablets of stone but on tablets of human hearts (2 Corinthians 3:2-3; emphasis added).

Notice that Christ is the author of the transformation. The Holy Spirit is his literary assistant, writing Christ's words on hearts. As these disciples of Christ received God's word, the Spirit carved Christ's commands into their soft pliable hearts. Their hearts were soft (flesh versus stone) so the word of God stuck and became permanent. This passage reflects a prophesy Ezekiel made five to six hundred years before Christ.

> And I will give them one heart, and a new spirit I will put within them. I will remove the heart of stone from their flesh and give them a heart of flesh, that they may walk in my statues and keep my rules and obey them... (Ezekiel 11:19-20; ESV).

The heart of stone that Ezekiel mentioned is the mind that is dead, insensitive, and unresponsive to God's word. It has been petrified by sin. People with this kind of mind become dead to God's voice and commands. They resist and rebel against God's word. However, when Christ regenerates (Titus 3:5) these hearts through faith and in baptism (Colossians 2:12), the heart of stone is removed and a soft, pliable heart is implanted. This heart is sensitive to God's teaching and has the desire to obey. The Holy Spirit becomes a perpetual resident within each disciple (1 Corinthians 6:19). His main function is to give disciples supernatural power to obey Christ as Lord (Ephesians 1:19-23). It's no wonder we can experience permanent transformation.

In his first letter to the Corinthian church, the apostle Paul drove home the necessity of walking in righteousness and the wonder of the transformation experienced by the Corinthians:

> Or do you not know that the unrighteous will not inherit the kingdom of God? Do not be deceived: neither the sexually immoral, nor idolaters, nor adulterers, nor men who practice homosexuality, nor thieves, nor the greedy, nor drunkards, nor revilers, nor swindlers will inherit the kingdom of God. *And such were some of you.* But you were washed, you were sanctified, you were justified in the name of the Lord Jesus Christ and by the Spirit of our God (1 Corinthians 6:9-11; emphasis added).

Paul's letters of recommendation were divinely written, giving the weightiest of evidence. His response was, "Your changed lives are all the proof I need to validate my ministry and message." To the world, the proof of Christianity is a believer's changed life. If Christ's word and Spirit do not restore marriages and empower parents to raise godly children, and if the gospel doesn't deliver people from addiction, sexual perversion, wicked dispositions, and foul language transforming them into Christ-like goodness, then from the world's perspective; what good is it? People are tired of religion. It doesn't work and it is useless. People seeking God desire his patterns and power to change them into something new. If transformation is God's plan for every believer, then why are we seeing so little of it today? Let's consider inadequate Christianity.

INADEQUATE CHRISTIANITY

In many circles the American church is missing the mark. To quote Michael Horton, "Survey after survey demonstrates that evangelical Christians are as likely to embrace lifestyles every bit as hedonistic, materialistic, self-centered, and sexually immoral as the world in general."[16]

SALVATION WITHOUT REGENERATION.

One reason for continued carnality of believers is that churches often promote salvation without regeneration. Surveys reveal four startling facts about the religious beliefs of most Americans, including Christians. The ramifications of these erroneous views are devastating. First, most believe the human heart is innately good and not evil (see Jeremiah 17:9), inferring that regeneration is not needed. Second, most people believe that when people die, all go to heaven and only the very bad are required to pay for their sin in some type of purgatory. Third, many Americans believe that all religions lead to the same God, thus eliminating the necessity of the cross of Christ. Fourth, most Americans believe Jesus sinned while on earth. These four lies distort the entire message of New Testament Christianity and create

16. Ronald Sider, "The Scandal of the Evangelical Conscience: Why Don't Christians Live what They Preach?" *Christianity Today,* Feb. 2005. http://www.booksandculture.com/articles/2005/janfeb/3.8.html. Accessed October 2017.

an American counterfeit that suggests that the cross of Christ, regeneration, and transformation are not necessary for eternal life.

Universalism, the belief that everyone goes to heaven, has permeated the American Church and the Social Gospel Movement, a proponent of universalism that started in the early 20th century, continues to thrive in church circles today. To describe anyone as spiritually lost or in need of conversion can be considered condescending, arrogant, exclusive, and something akin to coercion and manipulation. For the Social Gospel Movement, the cultural mandate (Genesis 1:26-28) has replaced personal evangelism. This view states God has called the church to do social benevolence and bring social justice to the world. The method of the mandate is to redeem the environment, as well as social systems and institutions (though not individuals) that create injustice and oppression. Changing the system unlocks the door to individual salvation, which supposedly sets the individual free to rise out of personal poverty and bondage. The social gospel produces a salvation without regeneration, thus making personal transformation impossible.

Brian McLaren, a leader within the *emerging church*, suggests that our mission is not primarily to get people into heaven but to get heaven into our world (a version of the social gospel). His proof text is a section of the Lord's Prayer, "Thy kingdom come, thy will be done, on earth as it is in heaven" (Matthew 6:10). A traditional interpretation would say Jesus is referring to Pentecost (Acts 2). God's Spirit comes down. Forgiveness of sin through the blood of Christ now allows God's Spirit to dwell within people, making obedience to our king possible on earth as Christ reigns from heaven.

Churches with good intentions can unknowingly stumble into a hybrid of this view. They attract good citizens from the community because the congregation works in the neighborhood, partners with social organizations, and provides a friendly environment to do the work of God. Mind you, this is not bad. But if human depravity and sin are not identified as the core characteristic of brokenness, then providing social services through the church can simply transfer their dependency from government programs to church programs. We must love people but we must also acknowledge their sin problem. The broken need to understand this reality too. Feeding the hungry should provide opportunities for relationship building, spiritual conversations, and hopefully a presentation of the gospel. If the needy accept the gospel, the *lost sinner* will have *true* salvation. Feeding the hungry is not the end but a means to reaching spiritually broken people "dead in their trespasses and sins" (Ephesians 2:1).

Jesus fed the hungry, healed the sick, and included the outcast. The Body of Christ should do the same. But Jesus priority was "to seek and save the lost" (Luke 19:10). The fact people will spend an eternity in hell should drive us into the neighborhood with food for the body and the gospel for the soul (2 Corinthians 5:14-21). Redeemed through the blood and transformed by the Holy Spirit, these new believers will rise above circumstances and collectively renovate their own neighborhoods one life at a time (Romans 8:37).

SALVATION WITHOUT DISCIPLESHIP

A second reason for carnality and a lack of transformation in the church is that leaders and teachers make salvation and discipleship mutually exclusive. They would say every believer should pursue discipleship but at the same time suggest that it's not required because discipleship is not linked to salvation. You can accept Jesus as Savior, so goes the logic, without having to accept him as Lord. You can be justified by the blood but sanctification (taking on Christ's character and mission) is optional.

Some who hold this view point to I Corinthians 3:10-15:

> By the grace God has given me, I laid a foundation as a wise builder, and someone else is building on it. But each one should build with care. For no one can lay any foundation other than the one already laid, which is Jesus Christ. If anyone builds on this foundation using gold, silver, costly stones, wood, hay or straw, their work will be shown for what it is, because the Day will bring it to light. It will be revealed with fire, and the fire will test the quality of each person's work. If what has been built survives, the builder will receive a reward. If it is burned up, the builder will suffer loss but yet will be saved—even though only as one escaping through the flames.

The argument goes like this: Any person is saved if they confess Jesus as Savior. Carnal Christians have no reward in Heaven because their life was built using "wood, hay and straw" (3:12). These works are burned up in the Judgment fire (3:13). Devoted Christians have rewards in Heaven because their life was built with "gold, silver, and precious stones" (3:12). These kingdom works endure the flames of Judgment, thus bringing rewards in Heaven.

There is another interpretation, however, that goes as follows: 1 Corinthians 3:10-15 is a metaphor about building Christ's church. Paul was warning both true and false teachers that their work as teachers or leaders will be measured on Judgment Day. Paul referred to himself as a skilled master builder who laid the foundation for the church at Corinth. This foundation was Jesus.

In this metaphor, since the foundation is a person then the building materials must also be people. The *wood, hay and straw* are believers whose faith is burned up in the day-to-day fiery trials of life (1 Peter 1:6, 7). Their expectations of the new life are not fulfilled, possibly due to hardship, persecution, loss, or disappointment. In an event, they walk away. The apostle John described our lives as great tribulations (Revelation 7:14). Paul also warned the disciples at Lystra, "…'we must go through many tribulations to enter the kingdom of God'" (Acts 14:22). Let's see how this interpretation works itself out in the following paraphrase of 1 Corinthians 3:12-15:

Verse 13: "Each one's [the teacher's, preacher's and, leader's] work [discipling of members] will become manifest, for the Day [life's fiery trials] will disclose it…because it [the work of teachers, preachers, and leaders discipling believers] will be revealed by fire [life's trials], and the fire will test what sort of work [quality of discipling members] each one [teachers, preachers, leaders] has done."

Verse 14: "If the work [discipling believers] that anyone [teachers, preachers, leaders] has built [disciples transformed into Christ's character and mission] on the foundation [Jesus' redemption, character, and mission] survives [members being faithful throughout life's trials], he [the teacher, preacher, leader] will receive a reward [discipled ones are in Heaven]."

Verse 15: "If anyone's [teacher's, preacher's, leader's] work [discipling believers] is burned up [believers who leave Christ due to their fiery trials], he [teacher, preacher, leader] will suffer loss [the unfaithful member goes to Hell], though he himself [teacher, preacher, leader] will be saved [Heaven], but only as through fire [teachers, preachers, leaders must also be faithful to Christ through their fiery trials to enter Heaven].

Verse 12: the "gold, silver, precious stones" are the resilient disciples of Christ, who if trained properly, can persevere through the fires of life. Fire does not destroy gold or silver but purifies them. God uses the fiery trials to burn off the dross creating a conquering faith that is fully devoted and effective for our Lord.

So, from the outset, it is essential that preachers, teachers, and leaders emphasize that salvation and discipleship are part of the *same package*. Staying saved is conditional (see John 8:31; 15:1-10; Romans 11:17-23; 1 Corinthians 15:1; Colossians 1:21-23; Hebrews 3:6, 12-14). We must maintain our faith, and saving faith works. Faith that does not work is dead (James 2:17). We are told to "...*work out* your own salvation with fear and trembling, for it is God who works in you, both to will and to work for his good pleasure" (Philippians 2:12; ESV; emphasis added). This daily "working out" consists, in part, of cooperating with God's Spirit to transform us into Christ's character and mission.

DISCIPLESHIP WITHOUT SALVATION

The third reason for carnality and a lack of transformation among Christians is the misconception that discipleship can occur without salvation. I had the privilege to spend some time with Joe Ellis before he died. I first met Dr. Ellis in graduate school at Cincinnati Bible Seminary. He wrote the two classic books, *The Church on Purpose* and *The Church on Target*. In one of our conversations, I asked what he thought would be the next big focus in Christianity. His answer shocked me. "The next big wave will be to re-evangelize the church." His statement was based on a survey he had done with six different denominations that identified marks of salvation. Dr. Ellis was staggered by the high percentage of regular attenders who demonstrated little proof of their salvation.

For example, if the church believes the purpose of the Sunday worship service is evangelism, the Sunday gathering will target the neighborhood *profile* in order to attract the neighborhood. Sermons will attract crowds and provide a new blueprint for life by focusing on the winning attitude, perseverance, dealing with difficult people, having a mission in life, how to have a happy marriage and successful kids, and how to be blessed financially. But these churches seldom if ever preach sermons focused on the gospel, repentance, righteousness, commitment, denying self, making Christ Savior and Lord, the flesh versus Spirit, overcoming temptation, sanctification, Heaven, or Hell. These topics must also be preached for transformation to occur.

Without an emphasis on these key doctrines, we are left with discipleship without salvation. Our guests conform to the new patterns but with only short-term change because they lack the Holy Spirit. Discipleship in the absence of salvation (regeneration of the heart) produces a religion of works and a false sense of security. Church attenders come to the "banquet" regularly and consider themselves "in, but they don't possess the robe of righteousness. Look what the king will say to them:

> But when the king came in to look at the guests, he saw there a man who had no wedding garment. And he said to him, "Friend, how did you get in here without a wedding garment?" And he was speechless. Then the king said to the attendants, "Bind him hand and foot and cast him into the outer darkness. In that place there will be weeping and gnashing of teeth." For many are called, but few are chosen (Matthew 22:11-14; ESV).

So, have we ever thought of ourselves as being God's letter to the world? People read us every day. How are we portraying the One who lives in us, Jesus Christ? Is the portrayal accurate? Distorted? Or unclear?

The Corinthian believers were far from perfect but their changed lives demonstrated Christianity to be true.

C.S. Lewis states:

> If conversion to Christianity makes no improvement in a man's outward actions then I think we must consider his conversion to be suspect. Fine feelings, greater interest, more religious knowledge mean nothing unless they actually make our behavior better. The world is quite right in judging Christianity by its results. Christ taught us to judge by results. When Christians behave badly or fail to behave well, we make Christianity unbelievable.[17]

---

17. C.S. Lewis, *The Complete C. S. Lewis Signature Classics* (HarperSanFrancisco, CA.: 2002), pp. 12, 110.

Application Questions

1. Which of the following aspects of the cost of discipleship was most challenging for you when you became a Christian? How can you help others better understand and apply these requirements as they come to faith? a) We must love Jesus more than our families and our own lives, b) We must be willing to take up our crosses and follow him, c) We must renounce all that we have to be Christ's disciples, d) We must count the cost before we decide.

2. What unique challenges do you, as a church leader, face in your efforts to be Christ's disciple? What strategies are you using to personally take on Christ's character and mission?

3. If an outsider were to audit your church's messaging, resource allocation, and programming, what would that person conclude is your church's definition of "discipleship?"

4. Who in your church best represents your "letters of recommendation?" What does their life communicate about your spiritual leadership?

5. What strategies are you using to encourage your congregation to take on Christ's character and mission?

Group Discussion Questions

1. When you became a Christian, which of the following did you view as the biggest hurdle: a) Loving Jesus more than your families and your own life, b) Willingness to take up your cross and follow him, c) Renouncing all that you had to be Christ's disciples, or d) Counting the cost before you decided?

2. Why are universalism (e.g., no one will suffer eternal separation from God in Hell) and pluralism (e.g., all religions point to the same God) such popular beliefs, even among Christians?

3. Think about yourself as being God's letter to the world. What are the three positive things that the letter most clearly communicates? What are the three negative things that the letter most clearly communicates?

4. Consider Philippians 2:12. What should it look like for you to "...*work out* your own salvation" (actions) "with fear and trembling" (attitudes) on a day-to-day basis?

5. What specific things do you need to do, stop doing, or do differently in order to begin communicating a more Christ-like message to the world?

CHAPTER 4

CHURCH TRANSFORMATION PROCESS

In our journey to Heaven, what are the key stations that enable us to be saved, to be transformed, and to become Christ's letter of recommendation to others?

STATION ONE: JUSTIFICATION & REGENERATION

"...our sufficiency is from God, who has made us sufficient to be ministers of a new covenant, not of the letter but of the Spirit. For the letter kills, but the Spirit gives life" (2 Corinthians 3:5, 6; ESV).

Paul made it clear that he was not a self-made man and that he didn't create the gospel. Paul was divinely commissioned on the road to Damascus (Acts 9:15, 17-19) and he was divinely equipped as Christ's apostle through the outpouring of the Holy Spirit, who revealed to Paul the mysteries of the new covenant.

The New Covenant

The Hebrew word *covenant* in the Old Testament means "to cut." The saying, "Let's cut a deal" originates with this Hebrew word. A covenant began with the cutting of an animal in two parts. The contracting parties then walked between the two cut parts declaring their pledges. In the Ancient Near East this blood covenant meant, "May this be done to me, if I don't keep my oath."

In the New Testament, the Greek word for covenant is *diatheke*. It refers to any last will and testament. At the Last Supper, Jesus declared that his sacrificial blood would begin the new covenant between humankind and God (Luke 22:14-23). Why the need for a new covenant?

The Letter Kills

The letter that kills is the Mosaic Covenant written on tablets of stone. The Book of the Covenant was the remaining Laws of God written down by Moses (Exodus 24:4). To remain in relationship with God, Israel was to keep God's laws to perfection. The Book of the Covenant (Exodus 24:7) pronounced a death sentence on Israel because they broke it and we too stand condemned because we've sinned (Romans 3:23; 7:9-11; Galatians 3:10). Sin means missing the mark, or falling short of God's standard. The perfect, holy, righteous law of God cannot save us; rather it makes us aware of our sin and need for a Savior (Romans 3:20; 5:20; 7:1, 8).

I remember an incident that happened when I was eighteen years old, after I had been driving for a couple of years. I was in a hurry that day and failed to come to a complete stop at a stop sign – though, to my credit, I did look both ways. A police office saw me break the law and proceeded to pull me over and give me a ticket. The first words out of my mouth were, "But, Officer, I'm a good driver. I've never been pulled over before." His response? "Even if you are a good driver, you still broke the law, so you've got to pay the fine. That's justice." Neither my good driving record nor the fact that I looked both ways mattered to the officer because I was legitimately guilty of breaking the law.

Even if good and decent people break God's law just once, they become as guilty before God as any murderer, liar, or cheater and must pay the price (James 2:10). God's righteousness demands justice. To go to Heaven, we must be perfect, righteous, without sin, good, and holy because these are the qualities of God. Sin brings two curses upon us: guilt and a diseased and corrupt heart. The only way to be healed of these diseases is to be justified through faith in Jesus Christ to be saved.

Justification Removes Guilt & Punishment

But now the righteousness of God has been manifested apart from the law, although the Law and the Prophets bear witness to it—the righteousness of God through faith in Jesus Christ for all who believe. For there is no distinction: for all have sinned and fall short of the glory of God, and are justified by his grace as a gift, through the redemption that is in Christ Jesus, whom God put forward as a propitiation by his blood, to be received by faith. This was to show God's righteousness, because in his divine forbearance he had passed over former sins. It was to show his righteousness at the present time, so that he might be just and the justifier of the one who has faith in Jesus (Romans 3:21-26).

The Greek words for "just," "justified," and "justification" are from the same word family and can be applied as "right," "righteous," and "righteousness." So, as we think about justification, we know it has something to do with righteousness. The root word in Greek, *dikaioo*, is a legal term that conveys a judge "declaring" a person righteous. With that judgment we have a right legal standing before the law of God and freedom from the law's penalty.

Notice the way God brings us into a right relationship with himself "apart from the law" (Romans 3:21). No one can be saved through good works. One sin brings guilt and condemnation (James 2:10). We become right with God's law through faith in Jesus Christ. It is a gift from God that brings unending joy! Jesus redeems us (Romans 3:24). That means Christ paid the price for our sin on the cross.

Jesus is our propitiation (Romans 3:25), meaning that he turned away God's wrath. The Bible speaks of God's wrath over 500 times. God's wrath is simply the result of God's holiness coming in contact with sin. When light comes in contact with darkness, light automatically destroys the darkness. Darkness and light cannot co-exist. Every morning the rising sun destroys the darkness. The holy God cannot co-exist with sin. That's why when God descended upon Mt. Sinai, the people could not touch the mountain or they would die (Exodus 19:12). Remember Uzzah tried to stabilize the Ark of the Covenant? Touching the Ark brought instant death (2 Samuel 6). God's holiness coming in contact with sin brings death. The holiness of God is called "…a consuming fire" (Hebrews 12:29).

But God's love moved him to pour out his wrath on Christ as he hung on the cross in our place. Through the work of Christ, God, the eternal Judge, declared to believers, "No more penalty for you." This is wonderful news. Christ's payment satisfies God's righteous requirements of his law (perfection). It removes our guilt as law breakers. By God's grace, through our faith, in our baptism, God imputes to our personal account the righteousness of Christ (Acts 2:38; Romans 3:22; Corinthians 5:21; Ephesians 2:8, 9; Philippians 3:9). God continually covers our sins and pays the price by depositing the righteousness of Christ into our personal account.

That explains how God can be both "…just and the justifier…" (Romans 3:26). Again, Jesus' blood was necessary because of God's nature. God is both holy and loving. In the category of holy, we might include the words righteous, pure, and just. In the category of loving, we might also include merciful, gracious, compassionate, and benevolent. The sacrifice of Jesus on the cross satisfied both attributes of God. His holiness demands sin is punished. His love desires a relationship with us. The cross of Christ fulfills both, therefore God is both just and the justifier.

Christ Saves Us from Hell

Few people talk about Hell, but Hell is a real place where sinners will spend eternity. Sinners who have broken God's laws get what they deserve because Hell is the penalty for sin. Paul wrote, "…the wages [penalty] of sin is death…" (Romans 6:23). Hell is described as a place of darkness (Matthew 25:30), severe punishment (Hebrews 10:28-29), pain (Matthew 13:42), intense fear (Hebrews 10:31), burning fire (Matthew 13:30), humiliation, shame (Revelation 16:15), torture, no physical sleep (Revelation 14:11), a pit (Revelation 20:3), a prison (Proverbs 7:27), and a place where the flesh is eaten by worms (Mark 9:44). Most significantly, it is a place of eternal separation from God (2 Thessalonians 1:9). Hell is a place without hope. It involves pain, remorse, anguish, desperation—the worst that we have ever faced in life—but without any possibility of relief. This accurate description of Hell should motivate us to want to share the news of salvation with others.

God didn't create Hell for people but instead for the angels that followed Lucifer's rebellion against the God of Heaven (2 Peter 2:4ff). Second Peter 2:9 explains that God rescues the righteous through faith in Jesus Christ, but those who remain in their sin and rebellion go to Hell. Our friends and family must understand the terrible state sin creates, and we are obligated to tell them. The love that God showed us compels us to tell them the truth (2 Corinthians 5:11-21).

You and I will never win anyone to Christ if we skirt the truth about Hell or avoid telling the shocking news that they are lost without Jesus. Why would people accept Christ if they believe they can go to Heaven by being good, or if they do not see themselves in danger of eternal Hell, in need of a Savior? When we accurately describe the eternal suffering, it serves as a significant motivation for those who are not in Christ to receive salvation.

In Rob Bell's book, *God Wins*, the author cannot fathom God's love allowing anyone to spend eternity in a Hell. He's right on that point. That's why God sent his only Son to earth to die for our sins. "The righteousness of God through faith in Jesus Christ..." (Romans 3:22). Jesus is the loving kindness of God (Titus 3:4).

The Spirit Gives Life

Back to 2 Corinthians 3:6: "...but the Spirit gives life." Paul explained that "the letter" (Old Testament) could never enable us to be obedient to God's word, but the Holy Spirit can and enables a transformed life (Romans 7:6; 8:3). The law was powerless to help us obey, but the Holy Spirit living inside believers, provides the power to live out righteousness (Romans 8:4).

This is an ENORMOUS difference between the New and Old Testaments. The "letter" (Old Testament) was divinely given but the words could not produce righteousness in us. In the "new covenant" (New Testament) the Holy Spirit inside each believer, provides the supernatural power to obey God's word. In conjunction with our obedience, God's Spirit begins to transform our characters to reflect Jesus more and more.

Regeneration: A Heart Transplant

Justification is an *objective change* in our relationship to God's Law. Regeneration is a *metaphysical change* that begins with God giving the believer a new heart. Both regeneration and justification occur simultaneously in baptism (Acts 2:38; Colossians 2:11-12). Regeneration means we are now able to obey God's will. In this heart transplant operation, the heart of stone—a soul hardened and calcified by sin—is removed and replaced with a heart of flesh; soft and yielding to God.

How does this work?

Let's look at Colossians 2:11-12 (ESV):

> In him also you were circumcised with a circumcision made without hands, by putting off the body of the flesh, by the circumcision of Christ, having been buried with him in baptism, in which you were also raised with him through faith in the powerful working of God, who raised him from the dead.

Repentance means we voluntarily change our minds toward sinful attitudes and behaviors. We recognize sin made us guilty and our hearts are spiritually corrupt. We now see the need to make Christ our Savior and Lord. Repentance is a prerequisite to baptism (Acts 2:38).

Being dead in sin, the person is buried in baptism (Romans 6:3). Christ now enters as the Great Physician. He circumcises the heart, cutting away sin that produces the filth, impurity, and infection of the desperately sick and diseased heart. Peter described it as being "…born again…" (1 Peter 1:3). Titus described it as the "…washing of regeneration and renewal of the Holy Spirit" (Titus 3:5). The Believers are "…created in Christ…" (Ephesians 2:10). We become "new creations" (2 Corinthians 5:17).

C.S. Lewis describes regeneration this way:

> God became a man to turn people back into the original image of God. We become a new man, not an improvement of the old. It's not like teaching a horse new tricks. It's like turning a horse into a winged creature. Once with wings it will soar over fences which could never have been jumped. In the beginning, the wings are simply lumps on the shoulders and you can't tell they're wings. It's not mere improvement but transformation. It is a change from being a creature of God into a son of God[18]

18. C.S. Lewis, *The Complete C. S. Lewis Signature Classics* (HarperSanFrancisco, CA: 2002), p. 13.

Regeneration is also described in Romans 6:1-4 as spiritual resurrection. The believer can now walk in newness of life (Romans 6:1-14).

STATION TWO: SANCTIFICATION

Now if the ministry that brought death, which was engraved in letters on stone, came with glory, so that the Israelites could not look steadily at the face of Moses because of its glory, transitory though it was, will not the ministry of the Spirit be even more glorious? If the ministry that brought condemnation was glorious, how much more glorious is the ministry that brings righteousness! (2 Corinthians 3:7-9)

Go back and read Exodus 34:29-35. When God descended upon Mt. Sinai it was a spectacular, fearful, yet glorious sight. The thick black cloud that encompassed God brought such an explosion it produced lightning, fire, smoke, and thunder; literally shook the entire mountain. Moses then climbed Mt. Sinai to receive the Ten Commandment tablets. Forty days later, as Moses descended, his face glowed so radiantly that Aaron and the people were afraid to approach. Moses had peered into the glory of God and it changed his physical appearance. The radiance faded the longer he was away from God's glory.

As spectacular as God's appearance, his dwelling with Israel, the giving of his written law on tablets of stone, and the transforming effect it had on Moses were, Paul explains that the Old Covenant does not compare to the greatness, power, and longevity of the New Covenant. The perfect law did reveal God's holy character but it also condemned humankind who failed to keep it. The glorious law did transform Moses, but the effect was temporary. When God came down at Pentecost, (Acts 2) he removed the believer's sins through the blood of Christ. With sins removed, God could dwell not on a mountain but in the hearts of his forgiven people. The power of the indwelling Spirit brings permanent and eternal transformation.

"Therefore, since we have such a hope, we are very bold. We are not like Moses, who would put a veil over his face to prevent the Israelites from the end of what was passing away" (2 Corinthians 3:12-13).

This truth makes us very bold. The Greek word translated bold (*parresia*) gives us our English phrase, "to go public."[19] Moses was not so bold. He veiled his face, not out of embarrassment that God's glory was fading from his face but to teach an eternal truth. This newly established covenant that related to God through obedience to his law was destined to fade and pass away. It revealed God's holiness, but men failed to obey it. The perfect law of God now condemned sinful man. Yet, because of God's love he created the new covenant that provided payment for sins through the blood of Christ and the indwelling of God's Spirit.

It's also interesting that Moses regularly entered the tabernacle to speak with God. Basking in God's radiant glory, Moses' face would glow again. After passing the information on to Israel, Moses would put the veil back on as God's glory would fade. Moses' actions communicated over and over again that this established order of relating to God was temporary.

"But their minds were made dull, for to this day the same veil remains when the old covenant is read. It has not been removed, because only in Christ is it taken away" (2 Corinthians 3:14).

Paul made the point that Moses' teaching, though repeated often, did not take root. The Jewish people were unable to acknowledge the need for Christ's blood to remove their sins. This veil that stops people from seeing the need for Christ may be ignorance, pride, tradition, or even idolatry. Only when a person comes to Christ is the veil taken away. Believers understand that Christ fulfills all the righteous requirements of the law. Salvation and reconciliation to God are provided through faith in the atoning work of the cross. The veil is taken away.

"Now the Lord is the Spirit, and where the Spirit of the Lord is, there is freedom" (2 Corinthians 3:17). In baptism, when Christ's Spirit enters the believer's life, He brings freedom from the eternal consequence of sin (Romans 8:1), but also freedom from sinful attitudes and behaviors. We experience permanent change. Another freedom we receive is we can boldly proclaim and radiate the life-transforming gospel. People can look at us and actually see God's glory radiating from our character, words, and attitudes. We show victory over sin through Jesus. We can also reflect God's holiness

---

19. William Baker, *The College Press NIV Commentary: 2 Corinthians* (Joplin, MO: College Press Publishing Company, 1996), p. 156.

to the world. How does God transform us?

The Process of Transformation

"But we all, with unveiled face, beholding the glory of the Lord, are being transformed into the same image from one degree of glory to another. For this comes from the Lord who is the Spirit" (2 Corinthians 3:18; ESV).

REMOVE THE VEILS

"But we all, with unveiled face..." The veil that must be removed in order to experience salvation and transformation is this veil of trusting in our own righteousness and good works to save us. No one can be justified and stand righteously before a just and holy God because we've all sinned (Romans 3:23). The good news is that while we all deserve punishment, "the free gift of God is eternal life in Christ Jesus our Lord" (Romans 6:23).

New Testament Scripture also identifies other veils that block salvation and transformation and so must be removed.

> When you follow the desires of your sinful nature, the results are very clear: sexual immorality, impurity, lustful pleasures, idolatry, sorcery, hostility, quarreling, jealousy, outbursts of anger, selfish ambition, dissension, division, envy, drunkenness, wild parties, and other sins like these. Let me tell you again, as I have before, that anyone living that sort of life will not inherit the Kingdom of God (Galatians 5:19-21; NLT).

Repentance means that we voluntarily change our minds toward sinful attitudes and behaviors. Notice Paul made it clear it is unacceptable to continue in sin and claim Christ as Savior and Lord. The apostle Paul said, "Shall we go on sinning so that grace may increase, God forbid" (Romans 6:1). Without a change in spiritual direction there is no salvation. The last sentence of verse 21 makes it very plain.

Sexual immorality refers to any sexual activity outside of marriage between a man and women. *Impurity* denotes a dirty mind. *Lustful pleasures* carries the idea of parading sinful behavior without shame. *Idolatry* is valuing a person or thing over God. *Sorcery* is using drugs to escape reality and responsibility. It also carries the idea of trying to control others by manipulating universal forces. *Hostility* comes from believing one is superior to other races, genders, or nationalities. It's a condescending, superiority attitude. *Selfish ambition* reflects strife, rivalry. It's ego-driven self-exaltation based on personal achievement, position, and talents. Daily we need to remove these veils as well as other sinful attitudes to allow the Holy Spirit to bring transformation.

CAREFULLY STUDY JESUS

"...beholding the glory of the Lord..."

The Greek word to behold is *katoptrizomai*. It means to peer with intensity, contemplate, evaluate, and even meditate as one looks. The idea is to see the detail in order to *reflect or change*. Every morning we peer into our bathroom mirror to clean up for the day. As Christians, we do the same with our spiritual life. James challenged us to "looks intently into the perfect law...and continues in it..." (1:25) and then act it out in our daily lives.

Many Christians read Scripture to be encouraged by the stories in the Bible where God helps his people with their daily problems. That's a good reason to read Scripture, but have you ever considered the Bible as the mirror in which we see God so that you might reflect him to the world? Remember you are God's letter of recommendation. Carefully study Jesus and Scripture to catch God's reflection so that you can "...put on the new self..." (Ephesians 4:24).

With our sins removed we can gaze intently into Jesus' reflection of God without fear. We study the image until it is burned into our soft new hearts. What happened to Moses when he physically radiated the effects of contact with God's holiness happens to believers spiritually. What happened to Moses on the outside should happen to us on the inside. The glory of God wonderfully changed the appearance of Moses and God's glory will change our inward appearances too.

GOD CHANGES US

"...are being transformed into the same image from one degree of glory to another. For this comes from the Lord who is the Spirit."

Our transformation is gradual and dependent upon how intently we study the "script" and learn to act it out. I use the term *act* because the words imitate and mimic are both theatrical terms for actors who learn a script and take on a new character. They work out the mannerisms, attitudes, and behaviors of the characters they're portraying on stage. When Harry Truman's daughter watched the movie about her father, the actor had so captured Harry's mannerisms and behaviors that she could be heard saying, "It's him, that's my dad." Gary Sinise the actor said that the granddaughter called him "grandpa." The director, Frank Pierson, was so captured by Sinise's attention to detail, he forgot it was Sinise and believed it was Truman. At one point the director leaned over and whispered, "Mr. President would you mind doing the line this way."[20]

We learn the script and act it out daily. The Holy Spirit actually takes our study and obedience and changes us into the image of Christ. C.S. Lewis wrote, "We must get over wanting to be needed. This is often the greatest temptation. To become a new person means losing what we call 'ourselves.' Out of ourselves into Christ we must go. His will becomes our will. We are to think his thoughts, to have `the mind of Christ'."[21]

If an actor can memorize a script the size of a Bible and practice working out the new character on stage, surely out of devotion and love for our Lord and Savior we can memorize his script and live him out on the stage of life, to be his letter to the world.

"Put on the Lord Jesus Christ, and make no provision for the flesh, to gratify its desires" (Romans 13:14; ESV). The phrase put on means we wrap Christ around us as we would a coat. The apostle Paul challenged the Corinthians, "Follow my example, as I follow the example of Christ" (1 Corinthians 11:1). "Therefore be imitators of God, as beloved children" (Ephesians 5:1; ESV). Everyone is a mirror. When someone speaks or acts out behavior they are reproducing what they've heard and seen. People are a

20. Susan King, *The LA Times*, "Acting Presidential: Gary Sinise Plays Harry S. Truman to the Last Detail in HBO Film". Sept 3, 1995. http://articles.latimes.com/1995-09-03/news/tv-41662_1_gary-sinise. Accessed October, 2017.
21. C.S. Lewis, *The Complete C. S. Lewis Signature Classics* (HarperSanFrancisco, CA.: 2002), p. 117.

reflection of their parents, teachers, homeland, politics, and more. Christians put off the old self. We learn the new script of Jesus, then we put on Christ.

C.S. Lewis says,

> Our true self is waiting for us in Him. The more I resist Christ and try to live on my own, the more I resist Christ and try to love by own heredity, upbringing, surroundings and natural desires, I actually loose me. I become dominated by other things. It's when I give myself up to Christ's character, that's when I begin to have a personality of my own. Nothing in you that has not died will ever be raised from the dead.[22]

METAMORPHOSIS

"...are being transformed..."

Jim Allen makes the analogy of regeneration and sanctification using the monarch butterfly. The caterpillar attaches to a tree and encases itself within a cocoon. The cells turn off one by one causing the larvae to slowly dissolve from its former state into an unrecognizable substance and die. Once the larva is dead, certain inactive cells within the "goo" that were present from birth turn on and begin to re-build a new creature completely unlike the former. Once the new creation, the new butterfly is ready, it begins to struggle to free itself from the cocoon. It is this struggling that creates the circulatory system that carries essential nutrients to the developing wings as they flex (struggle) against the wrappings of the cocoon. The struggle forces fluids into the legs and wings out of the body. Without the struggle the butterfly remains bloated with tiny wings and legs and eventually dies.[23]

The analogy of the butterfly has some true similarities to the process of regeneration and sanctification. As believers, we die in our baptism. Christ gives us a new heart (regeneration). We rise to live a new life. We are a new creation. As believers, our sanctification (discipleship) involves hard work and struggle. "...work out your salvation with fear and trembling, for it is God who works in you, both to will and to work for his good pleasure" (Philippians 2:12 ESV).

---

22. Ibid., p. 118.
23. Jim Allen, *Blogos*, "The Butterfly Effect: Transformation in the Christian Life". http://www.blogos.org/keepwatch/christian-life-transformation.php. Accessed October, 2017.

The struggle phase for believers is life. We study the script and put on Christ. The pains and problems of life can actually have a good effect on us. They prove the genuineness of our faith (1 Peter 1:7). They dislodge our loyalties from people or things and allow us to truly attach our identities to Christ.

Now can you see why our definition of church must be consistent with how Jesus defined the church? Church is not a place, a service, an event, or a location. Church is individuals and collectively God's children called out of the world to assemble, be trained, and be transformed to take on the mission of Christ, then to go out as his letters of recommendation and win the lost for Heaven. This is why we exist. This is our purpose on earth. Let's embrace it and be transformed.

Application Questions

1. How often do you find yourself striving to achieve, and evaluating yourself against, the unachievable standard of perfection? What factors most commonly drag you back into Law thinking?

2. Consider 2 Corinthians 3:6. In what ways have you experienced the life-giving work of the Spirit recently?

3. With what sense of urgency do you share the gospel with your family, friends, congregation, and neighbors? How do you incorporate sin, its consequences, and hell into those conversations? In what ways can you be more intentional about those conversations and transparent about their dire situation?

4. How does the justification you received through Christ continue to impact your understanding of God and your motivation to pursue transformation?

5. What parts of the "script" outlined in the Bible are most challenging for you to live out consistently? What factors contribute to those difficulties and what strategies are you using to stay on script?

Group Discussion Questions

1. What is the smallest, most insignificant, or inconsequential immoral decision you've ever made? What is the biggest, most significant or consequential immoral decision that a person could make? What does James 2:10 teach about the difference between those two sins?

2. Which of the following two people feels most relieved, and why? a) The innocent person who is acquitted and spared the death penalty or b) the guilty person who is acquitted and spared the death penalty. Which of these best describes our situation as we stand before God?

3. Which of the following best describes the typical person's life change after accepting Christ? a) 45 degree turn; they make a few cosmetic changes but none that are significant, c) 90 degree turn; they give up their prior way of life, just to land on another path that points away from God's will, or) 180 degree turn; they make a full turn away from their own ways to God's ways.

4. What are some reasons why a regenerated heart – no longer a heart of stone – is necessary in order to take on the character and mission of Christ?

5. In what ways could we reasonably expect that our neighborhoods would be transformed if Christians consistently modeled the character and mission of Christ?

TRANSFORMATION
through TRANSPARENCY

DAVID FAUST

CHAPTER 5

GRAB THE WINDEX:
THE VALUE OF TRANSPARENCY

t's hard to see through a dirty window.

That's where the Windex comes in. There are other brands of window cleaner out there, but I can always count on good old Windex when my windows are dirty. Who doesn't recognize its familiar ammonia-like smell and that bright shade of neon blue? (Would Windex work as well if it were a different color?)

So far no one has invented spiritual Windex, but it certainly would come in handy. How convenient would it be if church leaders could go to the store and buy a couple of bottles to keep on hand? When your vision gets cloudy, set the nozzle to spray and squeeze the plastic trigger. A few well-aimed blasts of blue liquid followed by some firm wipes with a paper towel, and everything would be clear again.

Unfortunately it's not that easy. Even if the church's vision is clear to you, it doesn't take much to muddy it up. A staff member proposes a new program that sounds exciting but would take your church in a different direction. An impatient volunteer attends a leadership conference and comes back with a great idea for transforming your church's small groups. But is this the Lord's leading or is it like Saul's armor—an idea that fit Saul, but didn't fit David? A long-time church member you thought was fully on-board with the church's direction expresses serious doubts in a public meeting. Vision is getting cloudy. Bring on the spiritual Windex!

Vision isn't the only thing that gets cloudy for leaders. What about relationships with others in the church? Do the members of your church truly know who you are and what matters most to you? Do they really know what makes you tick? What about your "Timothies"—the men and women you are seeking to develop as leaders? Do they wish they had some spiritual Windex so they could see more clearly into the windows of your mind and heart? How much have you shared with them about your struggles, failures, and dreams? Have you provided them a clear, unclouded line of vision into the lessons you have learned, the victories you have enjoyed, and the ways God has led you? How much *should* you share with them?

Transparency is rarely addressed in leadership literature, but it's a vital quality if we want to build Christ-centered relationships that transform lives.

Transparency—What It Means

Our word transparency comes from the Latin *transparentia*, which literally means "shining through." According to Dictionary.com, something is transparent if it is "made visible by light shining through from behind," so transparency is a natural concept for all of us who follow Jesus, the light of the world.

If anyone should be comfortable with transparency, it's a Christian. When you're transparent, you can say to others, "What you see is what you get." You can live in a way that communicates, "My life is an open book, and you are free to read the pages." God already knows everything written there anyway, and we have nothing to hide, so we can be real, honest, and authentic, opening ourselves to others without hiding the truth. Will Rogers quipped, "So live that you would not be ashamed to sell the family parrot to the town gossip."

Sometimes the expression, "I can see through you," is used in a negative sense. "I can see through your phoniness and pretense," or "I can see through the real motives behind your sales pitch." Christian leaders, however, should be examples of a positive kind of transparency that allows followers to say, "I can see what (and who) you really are."

We tend to resist self-disclosure because we don't want others to get too close, to see too much, to know us too well. But transparency is not narcissism—calling attention to ourselves. The goal is allowing others to see Christ in us.

Numerous examples of transparency appear in the Bible. God made himself transparent at Mount Sinai, revealing as much of himself as Moses could take in (Exodus 33:18-34:7; 2 Corinthians 3:7-18). David and Jonathan had a transparent relationship with each other, sharing such a deep bond of fellowship that they were "one in spirit" (1 Samuel 18:1). Jesus was transparent with his disciples, gradually revealing his Messianic identity and explaining to them in private the deeper lessons undecipherable by the crowds (Mark 4:33, 34).

Integrity was a hallmark of the apostle Paul's ministry. He believed in *financial transparency*. With him there were no shady business deals, no hidden agendas, no under-the-table arrangements that would result in his own personal enrichment. When entrusted with the church's offerings, Paul insisted, "We want to avoid any criticism of the way we administer this liberal gift. For we are taking pains to do what is right, not only in the eyes of the Lord but also in the eyes of man" (2 Corinthians 8:20, 21).

Paul also believed in *motivational transparency*. His motives for ministry were pure and authentic. He told the church in Thessalonica, "We are not trying to please men but God who tests our hearts. You know we never used flattery, nor did we put on a mask to cover up greed—God is our witness" (1 Thessalonians 2:4, 5). In what has been called Paul's most transparent letter (Second Corinthians), he told his friends, "For we do not preach ourselves, but Jesus Christ as Lord, and ourselves as your servants for Jesus' sake. For God, who said, 'Let light shine out of darkness,' made his light shine in our hearts to give us the light of the knowledge of the glory of God in the face of Christ" (2 Corinthians 4:5, 6). The light of Christ shone brightly on Paul's life, and in turn Paul shone the spotlight on Christ, not himself. He didn't need to be secretive or manipulative. Paul lived his life right out in the open, transparently pointing anyone he could to Jesus Christ.

Furthermore, Paul believed in *relational transparency*. His mentoring relationship with Timothy was characterized by remarkable frankness, practical advice, and spiritual depth. These men knew each other's emotional makeup. Paul knew Timothy's family. He was on a first-name basis with his young protégé's grandma and mom, Lois and Eunice (2 Timothy 1:5).

Paul and Timothy knew each other so well that they were aware of one another's travel plans and physical ailments. Paul felt free to give Timothy practical advice about how to deal with his stomach problems and frequent illnesses (Philippians 2:19-24; 1 Timothy 5:23). Timothy evidently shared openly with Paul about the details of his ministry and the challenges he faced as he led the church in Ephesus. In turn, Paul shared his own disappointments in ministry, including the way Demas abandoned him and Alexander the metalworker caused him great harm, and used these examples to teach and guide Timothy (2 Timothy 4:9-15). Paul challenged and encouraged Timothy when he saw areas where his apprentice struggled. These two men prayed for each other and poured out their hearts to one another. Paul even knew what made Timothy cry, and recalled the tears that were shed when they parted from each other (2 Timothy 1:4).

Transparent—Why?

Transparency can be risky business, but it's vital for Christian leaders. Here's why.

Transparency matters because truth and love matter. According to business guru Jack Welch, "The highest form of management is the truth." That comes as no surprise to those who lead churches, because truth is our main commodity. We preach it from the pulpit and lobby for it in the public square. Jesus prayed, "Your Word is truth" (John 17:17).

But truth has to be tempered and communicated with love. One mark of a healthy church is "speaking the truth in love" (Ephesians 4:15). Truth and love go together in Scripture because they go together in life. "Jesus Christ, the Father's Son, will be with us in truth and love" (2 John 3).

A healthy combination of truth and love is an essential tool in a leader's toolbox. John Neffinger and Matthew Kohut, who have studied what makes people compelling and influential, point out that influence is a combination of strength and warmth. They note, "Strength measures how much people can affect the world, and warmth shows how much people are concerned about our interests."[24]

Transparency matters because integrity matters. It's tempting for church leaders to think of truth as something "out there," when actually God wants it to be something "in here"—inside our hearts, something we live and breathe, not just a list of concepts we affirm. The Lord desires "truth in the inner parts" of our lives (Psalm 51:6). Someone has said, "What lies behind us and what lies before us are tiny matters compared to what lies within us."

Transparency matters because grace matters. We are not only saved by grace; we also must lead by grace. God's grace allows us the freedom to be transparent. If we really believe, as the songwriter said, "Nothing in my hand I bring; only to the cross I cling," then there's nothing to hide and no one to impress.

By grace, God gives us gifts to develop and deploy for his glory. By grace, God even redeems our mistakes, and the difficult lessons we learn in life become part of our equipment for helping others. Seeing yourself as a sinner saved by grace allows you to show mercy and "second-mile" kindness to others. In his book, *Unoffendable*, Brant Hansen points out, "I'm guessing, if you are driving home after being forgiven of a capital crime, you're going to let people merge in your lane without yelling at them."[25]

Transparency Has Its Limits

Let's be honest, though. For many leaders, the idea of transparency seems a little unnerving and even foolhardy—especially if you assume transparency means dumping your emotional garbage truck and pouring out every private thought and feeling. That would not be a smart move for a leader, nor would it reflect the kind of transparency we're talking about in this book. Transparency doesn't mean being completely unfiltered in the way you open your heart to others. Nor does it mean being naïve. Some people are unsafe. They gather information mainly to use it against you.

24. See John Neffinger and Matthew Kohut, *Compelling People: The Hidden Qualities that Make Us Influential* (Hudson Street/Penguin, 2013).
25. Brant Hansen, *Unoffendable* (Nashville: W Publishing Group, 2015), p. 65.

Here are some common sense limitations when it comes to transparency for leaders.

BIBLICAL CONSTRAINTS

Scripture warns us to be wise about what we say, when and how we say it, and with whom we share certain information. "He who guards his mouth and his tongue keeps himself from calamity" (Proverbs 21:23).

Transparency doesn't mean indiscriminately spilling your guts to others. Jesus didn't answer every question, grant every request, or accommodate every demand for his attention. He refused to perform miracles when a sign-seeking crowd requested them (Matthew 16:1-4). He refused to respond when Herod "plied him with many questions" (Luke 23:9). He remained silent when Pilate pushed him for information (John 19:8, 9). When his disciples insisted, "Everyone is looking for you," Jesus went off in a different direction (Mark 1:35-38). He wasn't trying to be obstinate or secretive; he simply remained focused and undistracted about his primary mission. Jesus was a wise steward of time, information, and energy. That should be our goal, too.

LEGAL CONSTRAINTS

In addition to biblical limitations, there are legal constraints on transparency as well. Ministers and elders are privy to confidential information. A member of the congregation may share personal information in a pastoral counseling session that no one else should know. A staff member may learn about personnel matters that the law and human resources protocol require must be kept strictly private.

Be smart. What you learn about others in confidence needs to be kept confidential, or others will lose confidence in you. What you write in an e-mail on your church-owned computer can be subpoenaed in a court of law. Along with the privileges of serving as a church leader comes the responsibility of handling privileged information wisely.

FAMILY CONSTRAINTS

Does transparency mean pulling back the protective veil so others can see not only your own struggles, but also those of your loved ones? How many of your family's foibles and failings should you share with others?

Your story is your story; but your wife's story belongs to her, and your children didn't sign up to be lifelong sermon illustrations. Be cautious about sharing information that might embarrass your family or subject them to unneeded scrutiny and misunderstanding. A wise rule of thumb is simply this: If you're going to share personal information about a family member, always ask permission first.

Early in my ministry, in a light-hearted moment while preaching one Sunday morning I spontaneously mentioned how a large bowl of peanut M & M's had disappeared from the desk in my office. I joked, "I guess the youth group got hungry and ate them all." Suddenly noticing a strange look on my wife Candy's face, I looked at her and blurted out, "Was it *you*?" She nodded, the congregation laughed, and my sweet wife eventually forgave me for calling her out as the culprit. Lessons learned: 1) Spontaneity in the pulpit isn't always a virtue, and 2) Embarrassing a family member is never good form for a preacher. (Just for the record, I have my wife's permission to share the above story in this book!)

THE HOLY SPIRIT'S CONSTRAINTS

Admittedly this is a subjective point, but we need to heed the promptings of God's Spirit who dwells in us. When sharing information with others, it's wise to pay attention whenever there's a "check" in your spirit. If you sense God-given hesitation, bite your tongue.

If you're unsure what to say, follow the adage, "When in doubt, throw it out." In the name of transparency, don't say something or share information you may later regret. "He who holds his tongue is wise" (Proverbs 10:19).

Transparent—With Whom?

So far we have considered what transparency means, why it matters, and its limitations. Here's another question: With whom should leaders be transparent?

WITH GOD

"In the beginning God" is always the right starting point. We shouldn't try to hide anything from the Lord—as if we could! Mark Twain observed, "Everyone is a moon, and has a dark side which he never shows to anybody." But there's no point in trying to hide anything from God. "Nothing in all creation is hidden from God's sight. Everything is uncovered and laid bare before the eyes of him to whom we must give account" (Hebrews 4:13).

That's why I like this prayer paraphrased from the writings of C. S. Lewis: "Lord God, when I pray, may it be the real 'I' who speaks, and may it be the real 'You' to whom I speak."

David said it well: "Search me, O God, and know my heart; test me and know my anxious thoughts. See if there is any offensive way in me, and lead me in the way everlasting" (Psalm 139:23, 24). We must be transparent toward the Lord.

WITH OURSELVES

We also need to be transparent with ourselves. Martin Luther said, "I more fear what is within me than what comes from without."

Remember the repeated exhortation of the Lord's brother James about the dangers of self-deception? "Do not merely listen to the word, *and so deceive yourselves*." "If anyone considers himself religious and yet does not keep a tight rein on his tongue, *he deceives himself* and his religion is worthless" (James 1:22, 26, emphasis mine). John wrote, "If we claim to be without sin, we *deceive ourselves* and the truth is not in us" (1 John 1:8, emphasis mine). Genuine transparency requires being honest with ourselves.

The book *Leadership and Self-Deception* relates the true story of how, during the mid-1800s, doctors in Europe were distressed to find that one out of 10 women who gave birth at Vienna's General Hospital were dying from a collection of symptoms nicknamed "childbed fever." Finally investigators discovered the cause of the problem. Doctors at the research hospital had been splitting their time between conducting research on cadavers and treating sick patients without washing their hands thoroughly in between. In other words, diseases were unwittingly being transmitted to healthy patients by the hands of their own physicians. The "healers" were actually spreading the disease! If leaders ourselves carry the disease of self-deception, how can we help others get well?[26]

That's why Stephen Olford said we should view sin like a speck of dust in our eye. "As soon as sin sets in," he said, "I must stop all activity and remove it at once, else I cannot see."

WITH THOSE WE LEAD

Sometimes church leaders say, "I love preaching, but I hate administration." (I have said such things myself.) However, administration itself is simply a form of ministry. *Administer* comes from the words "ad" ("to) plus "minister." Leadership in any form—administrative, pastoral, or otherwise—is always about moving ourselves and others toward effective ministry. That's why it's so important to be transparent with those we lead.

According to Alan Ahlgrim, emotionally healthy leaders widen the circle of communication depending on the level of trust they share with others, and what others need. Ahlgrim suggests we should:

- Be honest with all.
- Be transparent with some.
- Be vulnerable with a few.[27]

Jesus progressively revealed information to his disciples as their capacity to deal with it increased. One time he acknowledged, "I have much more to say to you, more than you can now bear" (John 16:12), and later he told his disciples, "Though I have been speaking figuratively, a time is coming when I will not longer use this kind of language but will tell you plainly about my Father" (John 16:25-31). As the Lord "administrated" his relationship with the disciples and moved them toward ministry, he gradually unfolded what he wanted them to know. He was transparent, but he didn't dump the truck on them all at once.

Some Bible students think Paul may have had poor eyesight— an idea suggested by the fact that he wrote with "large letters" (Galatians 6:11)—perhaps even a leftover problem after he was blinded on the Damascus

---

26. The Arbinger Institute, *Leadership and Self-Deception* (BK Publishers, 2002). 17-20.
27. Alan provides a more detailed explanation of this concept in Chapter 9.

road. But Paul's spiritual vision was 20-20. In Acts 20:20 he reminded his friends that he never hesitated "to preach anything that would be helpful to you." That's the goal: communicate whatever is helpful and needed—nothing more, nothing less.

Historians estimate that the apostle Paul became a Christian around the age of 30 and died as a martyr for the faith in his early to mid 60s. That means Paul (formerly known as Saul of Tarsus) spent only about half of his earthly lifetime as a follower of the risen Christ, while he spent the first half opposing the Christian gospel. It also means after becoming a Christian himself, Paul only had approximately 30 more years to serve the Lord Jesus before his life on earth was over. Time was precious to Paul. No wonder he considered it so strategic to pour himself into next generation leaders who would continue to preach, teach, model, and pass along the gospel to succeeding generations. No wonder he told Timothy, "And the things you have heard me say in the presence of many witnesses entrust to reliable men who will also be qualified to teach others" (2 Timothy 2:2).

In their book, *Growing Young*, authors Kara Powell, Jake Mulder, and Brad Griffin talk about "keychain leadership." They point out, "Whoever holds the keys has the power to let people in or to keep people out. Keys provide access to physical rooms, as well as to strategic meetings, significant decisions, and central roles or places of authority. The more power you have, the more keys you tend to possess." Keychain leaders, the authors contend, are church leaders who are "acutely aware of the keys on their keychain, and intentional about entrusting and empowering all generations, including teenagers and emerging adults, with their own set of keys."[28]

Do you want to develop next-generation leaders who are empowered to make a difference for Christ? Don't be a dirty window. Get out the Windex. Open up clear, unclouded sight lines into your heart and mind so others who look up to you can see the light God is shining on your pathway. Then, like Paul, you can say, "Follow my example, as I follow the example of Christ" (1 Corinthians 11:1).

---

28. Kara Powell, Jake Mulder, and Brad Griffen, *Growing Young: Six Essential Strategies to Help Young People Discover and Love Your Church* (Baker, 2016), p. 53.

Application Questions

1. Who are you most transparent with? What factors have allowed you to be more transparent with that person than anyone else? How has that level of transparency impacted your relationship with that person?

2. What factors tend to keep you from being transparent with your family, your peers, and your congregation? Does that lack of transparency negatively impact those relationships and, if so, how?

3. In what ways are you currently modeling financial transparency, motivational transparency, and relational transparency?

4. In what ways and in what circumstances should your role as a church leader prompt you to limit how transparent you are with some people?

5. Who are the next-generation leader(s) you are mentoring? How are you modeling transparency with those people?

Group Discussion Questions

1. What are the most significant risks associated with being transparent? What are the most significant benefits and opportunities that arise from being transparent?

2. Which of the following values provides you the strongest motivation to model transparency? a) Truth, b) Love, c) Integrity, d) Grace

3. Who has made the biggest impact on your life by being transparent with you? How did that transparency help you? How has it affected the way you model transparency?

4. In what areas of life are you most likely to fall victim to self-deception - failing to be transparent with yourself? How does self-deception negatively impact your transformation efforts? What strategies can you use to become more self-aware and honest?

5. Is it important to model transparency with God since He already knows our hearts? Why or why not? What strategies are most effective for being transparent with God?

CHAPTER 6

STICKY WORDS:
COMMUNICATING WHAT MATTERS MOST

Everyone talks, but not everyone communicates. Everyone uses words, but few use them strategically.

John F. Kennedy noted, "To lead is to be misunderstood." Many do not understand the burden of leadership, nor will everyone grasp and agree with the vision a leader casts. However, effective leaders understand the power of communicating what matters most. They use words like soldiers use weapons, like mechanics use tools, like chefs use seasonings. Effective leaders communicate with "stickiness"—their ideas stick in the minds of those who follow them.

How many words do you speak or write in an average day? Language experts who study such things estimate that the average person uses about 16,000 words per day. Over the course of an 80-year lifetime that's approximately 467 million words. I'm guessing that some of us say a lot more, with gusts up to a billion words over a lifetime, while the quieter folks among us may get by with only a quarter of a million words over a lifetime. Either way, it's an impressive number; but it's humbling to wonder, "Out of the millions of words I say, how many will be remembered after I am gone?"

Church leaders are especially concerned about words. Sunday after Sunday we preach the Living Word (Christ) and the Written Word (Scripture).

We teach classes, present devotional thoughts, and lead meetings. We write articles, letters, blog posts, and more e-mails than anyone can count. We often find ourselves in situations where someone asks us to "say a few words." Out of all those words we say over the course of a long ministry, what percentage will have a lasting impact on those who hear or read our ideas? Ten percent, perhaps? Let's not flatter ourselves! One hundred years from now it will be remarkable if anyone remembers two or three specific sentences we spoke.

Jesus' masterful use of language is one factor that makes him stand out as the Master Teacher. Talk about "sticky words"! Two thousand years after he walked the earth, Jesus' brilliant insights continue to stick in our minds. Think about:

- His parables and stories, including the Prodigal Son and the Good Samaritan.

- His pithy one-liners, like "Blessed are the peacemakers," "Do unto others as you would have them do unto you," and "It is more blessed to give than to receive."

- His prayers, like the Model Prayer in Matthew 6 and his prayer for unity in John 17.

- His extended teachings, like the Sermon on the Mount (Matthew 5-7) and his Sermon on the Bread of Life (John 6).

What Do You Want to Communicate Most?

Paul's relationship with the young leaders Timothy and Titus provides a model of mentoring and healthy communication. The grace of God allowed these men to share transparently with one another and to speak openly about any parts of their lives and ministries that God wanted to transform. Timothy and Titus could feel safe with Paul—safe to be themselves, safe to share their personal struggles, safe to ask tough questions that arose in the course of their service to Christ.

Leadership requires words. To instruct and encourage the young apprentices he was developing, Paul must have engaged in lengthy conversations with these men. If Paul were alive today, it's easy to imagine him using e-mail, texts, and social media posts to communicate with the churches and their leaders.

According to the apostle Paul, we should speak "only what is helpful for building others up according to their needs, that it may benefit those who listen" (Ephesians 4:29). Another translation of that Scripture passage indicates that our words "give grace to those who hear" (*New American Standard Bible*). What a concept—our words can be vehicles of grace! That's why Paul says, "Let your conversation be always full of grace, seasoned with salt" (Colossians 4:6), because like salt on food, gracious words make our listeners thirsty to hear more. Do your words bring "grace to your hearers"?

Timothy struggled with fear. Transparency rooted in God's grace allowed Paul to speak openly to Timothy about how God's power and providence could help him overcome fear. Paul helped Timothy understand that the Holy Spirit would enable him to live a new life characterized by "power, love, and self-control" (2 Timothy 1:7).

Another of Paul's young preacher friends, Titus, had to deal with hard-headed and divisive individuals in the church he led on the island of Crete. In those days the Cretans were known for their low moral character. Paul expressed the common viewpoint of his time when he quoted a comment from one of the Cretans' own poets. Epimenides, who lived about 600 B.C., said of his own people, "Cretans are always liars, evil brutes, lazy gluttons." (And you think God has called *you* to serve in a difficult ministry environment!) Paul added his own observation: "This testimony is true" (Titus 1:12, 13). How should Titus respond when he found himself surrounded by untrustworthy people—liars, evil brutes, and lazy gluttons? Paul told him to hold firm to the "trustworthy word" (Titus 1:9). "Teach what accords with sound doctrine" (Titus 2:1). "Avoid foolish controversies" (Titus 3:9). If you think you have your hands full in your ministry, would you like to have traded places with Titus? Words alone wouldn't fix everything that was wrong in a place like Crete.

Reinforcing Words with Deeds

We derive our word *influence* from the Latin *influere,* which means to flow in. Influence happens when a person flows into a set of circumstances or engages in the life of another individual or group. Jesus "flowed into" and influenced the lives of his disciples with both words and deeds. Luke tells us that he wrote his Gospel about "all that Jesus began to do and to teach" (Acts 1:1). The order is significant: Jesus' teachings flowed out of his deeds, and his actions reinforced his words. (For example, Jesus didn't just talk about prayer; his disciples often saw and heard him praying.) There was consistency and continuity between the Lord's words and his deeds.

Jesus called his original 12 apostles to preach and exercise spiritual authority, but part of his purpose in calling them was simply for them to spend time "with him" (Mark 3:14). Some lessons are *taught*, while others are *caught* by being around key influencers. Paul devoted himself to preaching and teaching, but he also shared his life with the disciples so fully that he could say, "You know how I lived the whole time I was with you" (Acts 20:18). He told the Thessalonians, "We were delighted to share with you not only the gospel of God but our lives as well, because you had become so dear to us" (1 Thessalonians 2:8). Paul shared deep, transparent relationships with other Christians. You can impress people from "up front," but if you really want to influence them deeply, you need to do it "up close."

Youth ministry expert Reggie Joiner tells youth leaders to imagine the day they retire from student ministry. They are standing up being recognized for their years of service, and three teenagers walk up to them and express their gratitude. Each of the teens finishes with this sentence: "One thing I learned from you that I'll never forget is . . . ." Joiner asks, "How would you want them to finish that sentence?"[29]

---

29 Andy Stanley, Reggie Joiner, and Lane Jones, *Seven Practices of Effective Ministry* (Multnomah, 2004), p. 123.

Life Lessons That Stick in Our Minds

What do you want to ensure others learn from you? What are the vital lessons you want others to remember as a result of your ministry over the course of a lifetime?

Eddie Lowen, lead minister of West Side Christian Church in Springfield, Illinois, says you "build the culture you want with the phrases you repeat." Here are some examples of sticky sayings he has used in his church:

- "Speak up—as long as you say it to the right person, at the right time, in the right way."

- "Visibility x Voice = Influence."

- "Beware those who compliment you at someone else's expense."

- "When evaluating people for your team, evaluate those around them."[30]

Bill Hybels wrote a book about axioms—short, pithy adages—memorable statements that encapsulate principles you want to emphasize to those you lead. Some of his sticky sayings include:

- "Get the right people around the table."

- "Speed of the leader, speed of the team."

- "Never say someone's no for them."

- "Every soldier deserves competent command."

- "Always take the high road."

- "Excellence honors God and inspires people."

- "Fight for your family."[31]

---

30. Eddie Lowen, *Christian Standard*, February 2017, pp. 57, 58.
31. See Bill Hybels, *Axioms: Powerful Leadership Proverbs* (Zondervan, 2008).

Here are some sticky sayings I have tried to pass along to others in my own ministry:

- "Let's be a first-century church for the twenty-first century."

- "Leaders need to be 'idrealists'—idealistic and realistic at the same time."

- "Ministry mainly boils down to two things: teaching the Bible and loving the people. Everyone needs to know God's truth, and everyone needs to be loved. Where else but in the church will they find both?"

- "My aspiration as a leader? Be a noble man, with noble plans, who does noble deeds" (from Isaiah 32:8).

Wise words don't have to be loud words. According to an old proverb, "You cannot train a horse with shouts and expect it to obey a whisper." NFL head coach Tony Dungy led the Indianapolis Colts to a Super Bowl victory in 2007, but he was known for seldom raising his voice to his players.

Paul didn't have to shout to get the attention of Timothy and Titus. He called them his spiritual "sons" and shared with them from his heart certain leadership axioms, called trustworthy sayings or faithful sayings in the pastoral epistles, which provide useful talking points we can use with anyone we're mentoring in Christian leadership.

Faithful sayings make deep spiritual truth easier to grasp. Because they encapsulate "the pattern of sound teaching" (2 Timothy 1:13), the Bible's faithful sayings can help church leaders "hold firmly to the trustworthy message" so they "can encourage others by sound doctrine and refute those who oppose it" (Titus 1:9). People today are fed up with slick marketing campaigns and silly slogans, but they are hungry for substantial nuggets of truth, lovingly delivered. Paul's example shows how "faithful sayings" can be part of the legacy we pass along to the next generation.

Faithful sayings stick in our minds. First-century Christians didn't own printed Bibles conveniently divided into numbered chapters and verses. Short, memorable truth-summaries helped them to recall the apostles' teachings, and they do the same for us.

More than 40 years ago I heard Bob Stacy, the founder of Christ In Youth (CIY) say, "Praise to him who specializes in the impossible." I've never forgotten that faithful saying. In a devotion prior to a class lecture, one of my seminary professors, Dr. Lewis Foster, said, "Everyone talks about being relevant. But relevance is not the only factor. We also need to ask, 'What is important?' If something is important, it will always be relevant!" That was a faithful saying. Because of Dr. Foster's comment, over the years I have made an effort to distinguish what is truly important to believe and do, not just get caught up in a faddish quest for relevance.

Faithful sayings overcome negative talk. There was a lot of *unfaithful* conversation going around when Paul wrote to Timothy and Titus. Negative talk can destroy a congregation, so Paul said to watch out for "myths and endless genealogies" that "promote controversial speculations rather than advancing God's work" (1 Timothy 1:4). Faithful sayings stand in sharp contrast to the "meaningless talk" (1:6), "old wives' tales" (4:7), "nonsense" (5:13), "controversies and quarrels about words" (6:4), and "godless chatter" (6:20) that were spreading through the church. Not everything people want to talk about is worthy of conversation. Paul didn't want Timothy to focus on what have been called "TBU"—things that are "True But Useless." Paul warned Timothy, "Don't have anything to do with foolish and stupid arguments, because you know they produce quarrels" (2 Timothy 2:23).

Five Faithful Sayings from Paul

Paul's letters to Timothy and Titus contain five "sticky statements"—five memorable truths the apostle identifies as faithful or trustworthy sayings.

1. *A saying about salvation.* "Here is a trustworthy saying that deserves full acceptance: Christ Jesus came into the world to save sinners—of whom I am the worst" (1 Timothy 1:15). In mentoring Timothy, Paul didn't start with a list of leadership techniques. He started by emphasizing the grace of God and Paul's own sense of unworthiness. "The worst of sinners"? Talk about transparency! Paul didn't brag about himself; he humbled himself. Before getting into the nitty-gritty of church leadership, Paul

stressed the importance of salvation because in his inspired mind, God's grace IS a leadership principle—and a foundational one at that.

2. *A saying about leadership.* After laying down the foundational concept of God's grace, Paul then turns to the leader's calling. "Here is a trustworthy saying: Whoever aspires to be an overseer desires a noble task" (1 Timothy 3:1). In First Timothy chapter 3 Paul is specifically addressing those called to be overseers—pastors, elders, shepherds of God's flock. He wants Timothy to be clear that this is a high calling, not to be taken lightly. It is a "noble task." One indication that a person is qualified for the task is that he "aspires" to it, senses God's leading for him to consider it, and possesses a holy, unselfish ambition to shepherd God's flock. In light of the difficult responsibility involved, those who consider accepting a church leadership role must carefully evaluate their motives and weed out any unholy desire for power, money, or self-benefit (1 Peter 5:1-4). Dwight D. Eisenhower stated, "A person who values privileges above principles soon loses both." A. W. Tozer said it well: "A true and safe leader is likely to be one who has no desire to lead, but is forced into a position of leadership by the inward pressure of the Holy Spirit and the press of the external situation."

3. *A saying about hope.* Paul's next "faithful saying" reminds us to be hopeful. He says, "Godliness has value for all things, holding promise for both the present life and the life to come. This is a trustworthy saying that deserves full acceptance. That is why we labor and strive, because we have put our hope in the living God . . ." (1 Timothy 4:8-10). Hope is one of the leader's greatest tools. In any group, the person who becomes the most effective leader is usually the one who offers the most hope. Great leaders understand the past, but don't live there. Driven by vision and a holy dissatisfaction with the way things are, they "labor and strive" to move their organization toward a better future.

4. *A saying about perseverance.* Leadership is hard, so Paul offers Timothy some sticky words about the need to endure over the long haul. "Here is a trustworthy saying: If we died with him, we will also live with him; if we endure, we will also reign with him. If we disown

him, he will also disown us; if we are faithless, he remains faithful, for he cannot disown himself" (2 Timothy 2:11-13). Perseverance is one of a leader's most important qualities. Endure! Don't give up! Here are some sticky words about perseverance that speak to my heart:

- "Are you willing to endure what you hate to achieve what you love?" (Lena Wood)

- "The man who moves mountains begins by carrying away small stones." (Unknown)

- "He who would leap high must make a long run." (Danish Proverb)

- "Nothing in this world can take the place of persistence. Talent will not: nothing is more common than unsuccessful men with talent. Genius will not; unrewarded genius is almost a proverb. Education will not: the world is full of educated derelicts. Persistence and determination alone are omnipotent." (Calvin Coolidge)

- "For every two minutes of glamour, there are eight hours of hard work." (Jessica Savitch)

- "I have brought you glory on earth by completing the work you gave me to do" (Jesus in John 17:4).

5. *A saying about God's grace.* Paul's final "faithful saying" brings us full circle, back to God's grace again. "He saved us, not because of righteous things we had done, but because of his mercy. He saved us through the washing of rebirth and renewal by the Holy Spirit, whom he poured out on us generously through Jesus Christ our Savior, so that, having been justified by his grace, we might become heirs having the hope of eternal life. This is a trustworthy saying" (Titus 3:4-8). Our ministries start with grace—like Paul, seeing ourselves as undeserving sinners saved by God's unmerited favor. And our ministries continue by grace—recognizing that the strength of our service lies not in righteous things we do, but in the power of the Holy Spirit at work in us.

When you sing "Amazing Grace," are you still amazed that the God of heaven would allow you to be his ambassador? The first-century church was "awful"—"Everyone was filled with awe" for God (Acts 2:43)! Are you an "awe-ful" leader? When you think about what the Lord has done for you, does his grace still make you fall on your face in humble worship that stirs your heart to say, "Awww"? Under Christ's new covenant, ministry springs from grace, not guilt. Awe for the Lord is like rocket fuel that propels us forward and upward in service to our King.

Yes, words matter—especially for leaders. Let's use them wisely, intentionally, and strategically. You're going to say a lot of words over the course of your lifetime, but only a tiny fraction of what you say will actually be remembered. What sticky words—"faithful sayings"—do you want to instill in those you lead?

Application Questions

1. What are the three most strategic and effective ways that you use communication (e.g., written, spoken, or otherwise) to influence people?

2. In what ways does your ministry role make it easier for you – as compared to other people – to influence through words? In what ways does your ministry role make it more difficult for you to influence through words?

3. What leader behaviors must you model in order to give credibility to your words? What behaviors must you avoid because they would undermine your message and your integrity?

4. What are some specific ways that you would like to improve the content and/or effectiveness of your communication? What strategies and tools do you need to use in order to experience that growth?

5. When you retire, what do you want people to remember about your ministry, and specifically about the way you influenced people?

Group Discussion Questions

1. Think of the person in your life that has made the biggest impact on your walk with Christ. What is the thing you remember most about that person's influence? What was the single most impactful thing they said to you?

2. Think about the approximately 500 million words you'll use over the course of your life. Have you coined a term, phrase, or concept that will be remembered 50 years from now? What one sentence would you want people to remember?

3. Do you communicate most effectively in writing, speech, or action? How does this fact affect how and when you share information? Does it inhibit you in any way or is it an asset? Why?

4. How do actions impact the way other people hear, respond to, and remember words? Why are these considerations important for Christians as they attempt to influence their neighbors for Christ?

5. What would you identify as the top 5 rules for effective communication? How does each one contribute to your ability to influence others?

CHAPTER 7

LEADING FOR LIFE-CHANGE:
TRANSPARENCY THAT LEADS TO TRANSFORMATION

My wedding ring fit perfectly when Candy and I got married in 1975, but in recent years my ring seems to have shrunk a bit. Actually my fingers and joints have gotten a little bigger, so the ring became too tight. I eventually went to a jeweler to ask if my ring could be resized. He said "yes," and one week and a modest fee later, I was back to pick it up. I asked the jeweler, "Do you mind telling me how you did this?"

He answered with a question: "Do you really want to know?"

I nodded, and he explained the process. "First," the jeweler explained, "I cut the ring in half." I gulped. I had trusted one of my most valuable earthly possessions to a complete stranger, and the first thing he did was cut my wedding ring in half!

The jeweler went on. "After cutting it in half, then I added some gold and soldered the whole thing back together and polished it. That was it!" (The process didn't seem like a big deal to him.)

I said, "But when I look at the finished product, I can't see that you did anything at all." The jeweler shrugged his shoulders and said, "If you could tell what I did by looking at the ring, that would mean I didn't do a very good job."

I was amazed by the jeweler's skill—and his courage, to cut up someone's wedding ring even though he knew he had the ability to put it back together again.

Make no mistake about it: The Lord is more skillful than any jeweler. He is a master craftsman—the expert in making things new. He knows how to take our lives apart and put them back together again. Leadership is about transformation, and before God involves us in the transformation process for others, he begins by transforming our own hearts and habits.

Becoming a More Transparent Leader

Are you willing to become more transparent as a leader? As the jeweler did with my wedding ring, are you willing to allow God to take you apart so he can put you back together again in the way that he desires?

TRANSPARENCY IN YOUR PERSONAL RELATIONSHIP WITH GOD

According to J. Oswald Sanders, "Great leaders in the Bible were great because they were great in their praying. They were not leaders because of brilliancy of thought, because they were exhaustless in resources, because of their magnificent culture or native endowment, but because, by the power of prayer, they could command the power of God."

Prayer can be puzzling, though. Jesus said the Father in heaven already knows your needs before you ask him (Matthew 6:8). So what's the point of praying? What if I were to say, "My wife already knows what's going on in my life, so what's the point of talking to her?" Conversation with my wife isn't merely for sharing information. Steady, open communication nurtures our relationship and helps us understand each other more deeply. Likewise, the purpose of prayer isn't to inform God about details he already knows, but to nurture our relationship with him, seek his perspective, and invite his participation in our lives. Through prayer we participate in the Lord's transformation process, saying, "Shape my thinking about this issue, Lord. Guide my thoughts. Align my heart with your vision."

For many years I have kept on my desk a leadership prayer I learned from H. B. London: "O God, stretch my mind. O God, sensitize my conscience. O God, stimulate my courage."

Leaders need to develop not only our private prayers, but our public prayers as well. Preachers rightly pay a lot of attention to the preparation, content, and delivery of our sermons; but how much attention do we pay to the prayers we say in public settings? Many of us might be surprised to discover how carefully the members of our churches actually listen to the prayers we utter from the stage. Public prayers provide opportunities for spiritual transparency at its best.

The "pastoral prayer" seems like a lost art today, but it can still be a useful tool for spiritual leadership if we choose to reclaim it. Without any forethought earlier in the week, our public prayers tend to be shallow and trite; but with a bit of preparation, the pastoral prayer can become a moment to model transparency and a shepherd's love for the flock. Most congregations would welcome a short segment in the worship service where a minister of the gospel or a caring elder sincerely, thoughtfully, and with ample preparation ahead of time, prays from his heart, bringing the church family's burdens, cares, joys, and requests to the throne of God.

Spiritual transformation begins with the leader's own relationship with the Lord.

TRANSPARENCY WITH YOUR FAMILY, FRIENDS, AND COWORKERS

If anyone can spot phoniness in a Christian leader, it's our own family and friends. But how transparent should we be with the folks who live and work with us on a daily basis? How much information should a church leader share with his wife and kids when the ministry isn't going well or a person in the church is driving us crazy?

Here's a little axiom I have found helpful: **Share what you *must* with those you *trust*.** What "must" you share with family members and coworkers? Who is worthy of your "trust" with this information? Transparency must be tempered by good judgment. Have you developed a reservoir of trust that's deep enough and strong enough to bear the information you reveal? Whatever you cannot share with other human beings, you can lift up to the Lord in prayer.

Never whitewash the truth, but don't shroud it in darkness either. When deciding what to share with others, you don't have to "sugar-coat" things to make them look superficially rosy, but to coin a phrase, you don't have to "vinegar-coat" things, either. Some leaders try to make situations look better than they are, but others go around with such a worried, sour, negative attitude that they make things look worse than they are.

Those we lead need to hear two things in combination: "Here is the unvarnished truth," and "This is why there is still hope." Leaders have to be both truth-tellers and hope-givers. Isn't that exactly what God does? He always tells us the unvarnished truth. Yet, no matter how complicated or distressing the situation, he always offers hope.

If you're a parent, there may be times when you have to communicate unpleasant realities to your children. "We're moving to a different state." "Grandpa died last night." "Mom had a car accident." You can impart truth without destroying hope. That's also the case if you're a preacher announcing to the congregation, "We're not making our budget and we need to increase our giving," or a boss telling an employee, "We have to let you go."

The Lord can shape us into more transparent leaders with our families, friends, and coworkers. Share what you must with those you trust.

TRANSPARENCY IN YOUR PREACHING

My preaching has become more transparent through the years. When I was in my twenties and serving in my first ministry, a vocal critic in my church would frequently tell me, "Your sermons sound like academic lessons. You need to show more heart!" Week after week, the criticism was the same, and those words really stung, because the vocal critic who voiced them was my wife!

She was right. As a young man I was an eager student of the Scriptures. I enjoyed learning about the Bible from my seminary professors. The problem was, the people listening to my sermons didn't always appreciate the subtle nuance of a Greek word used in the New Testament. It wasn't that my listeners were hard-hearted or unintelligent. It's just that they were distracted. They were struggling to make ends meet on inadequate paychecks. Their kids were rebellious. Their bodies ached. Their bosses were demanding. Their marriages were struggling. Yes, they needed deeper appreciation for the meaning of the biblical text, but they also needed encouragement and hope. They needed to know how God's truth intersected with their lives, not just on Sunday morning but also on Wednesday afternoon and Friday night.

Our listeners need us to help them experience "Immanuel Moments," times when they recognize that "God is with us." To communicate well at the level of the soul, our hearers need to recognize that we understand their questions; we care not only about their forever future, but also about their day-to-day struggles. They need us to be transparent in our preaching.

Our church engaged in a series of studies and discussions on emotionally healthy spirituality, and one of my personal assignments was to preach a message called "Expanding Your Soul Through Grief and Loss." Weeks ahead, every time I thought about that sermon title I cringed inside. Something inside of me didn't want to preach on that topic. Who wants to come to church and hear about "grief and loss"? A lot of people, actually. When I finally gathered my thoughts, summoned my courage, and made the decision to preach with transparency and share what the Lord has taught me through my own struggles, the task became more doable. I admitted to the congregation that, because of the stubbornness of my own heart, many times the main avenue God has used to transform my soul has been the pathway of suffering. By being transparent about my own sorrows and disappointments, I was able to validate the difficult experiences others in the congregation have been going through and point them to the God of grace who can use grief and loss to enlarge our souls. Transparency leads to transformation.

Steps in the Transformation Process

The apostle Paul's admonition to Timothy is well-known: "Don't let anyone look down on you because you are young" (1 Timothy 4:12). I especially liked that verse when I was young. The *King James Version* puts it, "Let no one despise thy youth." I didn't want anyone to despise me! I remember thinking, "Yeah, you older people need to treat me with respect even though I'm young!" Recently it hit me: I'm now at an age where I need to be careful I'm not the one who does the despising! Those of us with decades of ministry experience under our belts need to be welcoming, respectful, and encouraging toward the young leaders coming up behind us. And we need to remain open to God's transformational work in our lives no matter how old we become.

A few verses later, Paul wrote, "Do not rebuke an older man harshly, but exhort him as if he were your father. Treat younger men as brothers, older women as mothers, and younger women as sisters, with absolute purity" (1 Timothy 5:1, 2). Spiritual transformation is an inter-generational process. Paul assumed there would be regular, respectful interaction between different generations in the church.

In his letter to Titus, Paul again stressed the value of inter-generational ministry. Older men? They should be "temperate, worthy of respect, self-controlled, and sound in faith, in love and in endurance." Older women? They should be "reverent in the way they live, not . . . slanderers or addicted to much wine." Young people? They should be "self-controlled" (Titus 2:2-6). The Lord calls each generation, young and old, to set a positive example and show honor to those in other generations.

Jesus began his ministry when he was about 30 years old (Luke 3:23). He was a young adult—a "Millennial"—when he went around preaching, teaching, and developing other leaders. Today I'm nearly three times as old as I was when I began my ministry, but I still have a lot to learn about transformative leadership. Here are four steps God has taught me about the transformation process for church leaders.

1. *Step from inadequacy to competence (but not overconfidence).*

Deep down, many leaders are insecure and feel inadequate. We know our weaknesses, our unholy thoughts, moods, and habits, and the temptations to which we are vulnerable. The truth is, we actually ARE inadequate to be ambassadors of Almighty God! Who is worthy of such a role? We can't claim any credit for ourselves, says the apostle Paul, "but our competence comes from God. He has made us competent as ministers of a new covenant" (2 Corinthians 3:5, 6).

What steps are you taking to grow in your competence as a leader? If we want our followers to grow, we need to keep increasing our own skill levels as well. Great leaders are usually first great learners.

According to Psalm 78:72, David shepherded the people of Israel "with integrity of heart; with skillful hands he led them." Both "integrity of heart" and "skillful hands" were important for David's leadership. Integrity mattered most, but skill mattered, too. If he didn't know how to sling stones, organize armies, fight battles, and write worship songs, he wouldn't have exerted so much impact. Likewise, Paul exhorted Timothy, "Devote yourself to the public reading of Scripture, to preaching and teaching," so that over time "everyone may see your progress" (1 Timothy 4:13, 15). At every age, God calls us to keep making progress as leaders. It honors the Lord when we keep improving our skills and getting better at what we do. I will never be fully "adequate" as a preacher of the gospel, but I want to be a more skillful communicator and leader in five years than I currently am now.

Will we sometimes have to lead out of weakness rather than strength? Of course! Will we still have to deal with those pesky thorns in the flesh? Of course! But like Paul, we can embrace the Lord's reassuring promise, "My grace is sufficient for you, for my power is made perfect in weakness" (2 Corinthians 12:9).

2. *Step from striving for personal success to helping others succeed.*

The leader's main objective isn't to call attention to himself, but to develop other people. Wayne Cordiero is right when he says, "Our problem is not a lack of leaders; it's an overabundance of undeveloped leaders."

I don't like to admit it, but as a young leader I was overly focused on my own personal goals: pursuing my education, writing articles and books for publication, sharpening my speaking skills. The older I get, the more I appreciate the wisdom in this quote from Jack Welch: "Before you are a leader, success is all about growing yourself. When you become a leader, success is all about growing others."

For years I have believed that my calling in life is to bear maximum fruit for the Lord. In recent years I have begun to understand that some of the fruit of my life may grow on someone else's tree.

The man who was my family doctor for many years decided to retire, so he sent out a letter informing all of his patients. I sent him a letter in return, thanking him for caring for me, my family, and many other patients through the years. He sent me back a note that said, "While I am looking forward to retirement, and the increased time and decreased stress it will bring, I feel incredibly blessed. I always felt like a pastor with a stethoscope. It became my clerical 'collar.'" No wonder he was a good doctor! His career goal wasn't just to make money or make a name for himself. He saw himself as "a pastor with a stethoscope." In any career or calling, it brings God glory when we make it a priority to care for others.

Which brings you greater fulfillment—preaching an effective sermon yourself, or listening to an effective sermon from someone you taught to preach? Reggie Joiner puts it bluntly: "You have only one of two choices: (1) You can desperately hold on to your job until someone inevitably replaces you. (2) You can prepare someone to do what you do and strategically replace yourself."[32]

May God give us the maturity to guard against pride, find joy in helping others succeed, and genuinely "rejoice with those who rejoice" (Romans 12:15). A Chinese proverb puts it this way: "When the work of the best rulers is done, their task accomplished, the people all remark, 'We have done it ourselves.'"

3. *Step from the brink of quitting to accepting perseverance as the norm.*

If a poll were taken of Christian leaders and everyone responded honestly, we might be amazed to discover how frequently many preachers, elders, and staff members consider resigning from their posts. Some of us dive into leadership assuming it will be fun and rewarding, only to learn over the course of a lifetime that the reality is, "To lead, you bleed."

One of Paul's toughest instructions to Timothy may have been when he told the young preacher to "stay there in Ephesus" (1 Timothy 1:3), because Ephesus was a hard place to serve, and there must have been many days when Timothy felt like giving up. Leadership is hard and perseverance is required not just occasionally, but daily. Lest we feel sorry for ourselves more than we should, let's remember that church leaders are not the only ones who are tempted to quit. Consider the

---

32. Andy Stanley, Reggie Joiner, and Lane Jones, *Seven Practices of Effective Ministry* (Multnomah, 2003), page 158.

perseverance demonstrated by a hardworking farmer, a career military officer, a lifelong school teacher, a stay-at-home mom, and the years of training and sacrifice involved in being a doctor or nurse.

A video documentary called *Dying Laughing* reveals that even comedians who make people laugh for a living usually succeed only after years of sacrifice and perseverance. Jerry Seinfeld observes, "Comedy is purely the result of the ability to withstand self-torture. That's how you get great comedy. You have to be willing to keep telling the same stupid joke 85 times over the course of many years. If you're willing to do that, that's how great jokes get written."

Notice Paul's repeated words of encouragement to Timothy about the need to persevere in his faith and in his ministry:

- "Watch your life and doctrine closely. Persevere in them, because if you do, you will save both yourself and your hearers" (1 Timothy 4:16).

- "Pursue righteousness, godliness, faith, love, endurance and gentleness" (1 Timothy 6:11).

- "Take hold of the eternal life to which you were called when you made your good confession in the presence of many witnesses" (1 Timothy 6:12).

- "Keep this commandment without spot or blame until the appearing of our Lord Jesus Christ" (1 Timothy 6:14).

- "Timothy, guard what has been entrusted to your care" (1 Timothy 6:20).

- "Join me in suffering for the gospel, by the power of God" (2 Timothy 1:8).

- "What you have heard from me, keep as the pattern of sound teaching, with faith and love in Christ Jesus. Guard the good deposit that was entrusted to you—guard it with the help of the Holy Spirit who lives in us" (2 Timothy 1:13, 14).

- "You then, my son, be strong in the grace that is in Christ Jesus" (2 Timothy 2:1).

- "Endure hardship with us like a good soldier of Christ Jesus" (2 Timothy 2:3).

- "Continue in what you have learned and have become convinced of" (2 Timothy 3:14).

- "But you, keep your head in all situations, endure hardship, do the work of an evangelist, discharge all the duties of your ministry" (2 Timothy 4:5).

Perhaps you have heard the story of how Corrie Ten Boom and her sister, Betsy, were imprisoned by the Nazis during World War II and transferred to the worst prison camp imaginable. The barracks where they lived were overcrowded and infested with fleas. The first morning they were there, they read in their Bibles where it says, "Give thanks in all circumstances" (1 Thessalonians 5:18). Betsy told her sister Corrie to stop and thank God for every detail of their living quarters. But at first, Corrie refused. How could she give thanks for their flea-infested barracks? But eventually Corrie gave in, and even though it didn't make sense, in her prayers she thanked the Lord even for the fleas. During the months they spent in the prison camp, Corrie and Betsy were surprised to find how openly they were able to hold Bible study and prayer meetings without interference from the guards. Several months later they learned the reason why: The guards wouldn't enter the barracks because of the fleas! God turned their misery into a blessing.

Perseverance requires what business leader Jim Rohn calls "disciplining our disappointments"—using our failures as stepping stones. Disappointments actually can spur us on toward greater accomplishments. Since leadership requires pushing toward positive change, if no one feels disappointed with us, we may not be leading at all. The author of *Canoeing the Mountains*, Tod Bolsinger, suggests, "Leadership is disappointing your own people at a rate they can absorb."[33] Someone quipped, "A good leader is doing his job when half the people are following him and half are chasing him."

The apostle Paul serves as an impressive example of perseverance.

---

33. For an insightful resource on navigating church change, see Tod Bolsinger, *Canoeing the Mountains: Christian Leadership in Uncharted Territory* (IVP Books, 2015).

As his life and ministry moved toward the end, he could say with confidence that he had fought the good fight, finished the race, and kept the faith (2 Timothy 4:7). Paul persevered because he was convinced, "The Lord will rescue me from every evil attack and will bring me safely to his heavenly kingdom" (2 Timothy 4:18). Don't you want to finish well, as Paul did?

In his book, *Stuck! Navigating the Transitions of Life & Leadership*, Terry B. Walling identifies five choices that make a Christ-follower finish well:

(1) *Mentoring*: Don't just lead others. Make the choice to allow others to speak into your life and shape you as well.

(2) *Spiritual Renewal*: Make the choice to seek God repeatedly and with passion.

(3) *Life-long Learning:* Make the choice of self-care and becoming a learner in every stage of your life.

(4) *Perspective:* Make the choice to live and reorient your direction based on God's sovereign perspective.

(5) *Calling:* Make the choice to allow God's will and call to be dynamic and unfolding throughout the course of your life.[34]

Here is one more step God uses to transform Christian leaders.

4. *Step from the status quo to God's preferred future.*

Without constant vigilance, the church tends to slip into maintaining the here-and-now instead of pursuing what-could-be.

Why did Paul find it necessary to remind followers of Christ, "Set your hearts on things above"? Why did he repeat almost the same exact words in the very next verse, except this time saying, "Set your minds" instead of "Set your hearts" (Colossians 3:1, 2)? Didn't the Colossian Christians already understand the concept of being "eternity-driven" rather than "this-life focused"? Evidently not. One of the jobs of a Christian leader is to constantly remind ourselves and those we lead that "our citizenship is in heaven" (Philippians 3:20).

---

34. Terry B. Walling, *Stuck! Navigating the Transitions of Life & Leadership* (LeaderBreakThru, revised edition 2015), p. 115.

The eternal God stands outside of time. We don't. But we can discipline ourselves to serve each day in light of God's forever priorities. The more we think beyond the limits of the calendar and the clock and see life from God's perspective, the more satisfying and purposeful our ministries will become.

The month of January is named after the Roman god Janus, who was often represented as having two faces—one that faced forward and one that faced backward. Christians look both directions. We look back and see God's faithfulness, and we look forward to the future with hope.

It's important to look back. Remember Paul McCartney's song, "Yesterday"? Supposedly it has been played on the radio more times than any other song in history. Remember how it starts? "Yesterday, all my troubles seemed so far away." McCartney said in an interview that when he wrote the lyrics, his first attempt at the first line said, "Scrambled eggs, oh my baby how I love your legs." Good thing he tried again and wasn't satisfied with his first attempt! "Yesterday" is a sad song. Any guy who's ever had problems with a girlfriend can relate to it. "Why she had to go, I don't know. She wouldn't say. I said something wrong, now I long for yesterday."

But it's not enough to whine about or long for "yesterday." Ecclesiastes 7:10 urges, "Do not say, 'Why were the old days better than these?' For it is not wise to ask such questions." We can learn from yesterday, but the things that remain relevant in every age are "faith, hope, and love" (1 Corinthians 13:13)—and all three of those qualities challenge the status quo. Faith causes us to trust God for blessings yet unseen. Hope moves us to look forward to God's unfolding promises. Love stirs us to sacrifice for people and causes we consider more important than our own immediate self-interest.

Remember the Lord's message to the people in Isaiah's day? "Forget the former things; do not dwell on the past. See, I am doing a new thing! Now it springs up; do you not perceive it?" (Isaiah 43:18, 19). Paul looked back, but he also looked forward. He said, "Forgetting what is behind and straining toward what is ahead, I press on toward the goal" (Philippians 3:13, 14).

Some nagging dissatisfaction is necessary equipment for Christian leaders. Things won't change for the better until you get tired of the way things are. When Goliath terrorized the army of Israel, David said, "Why doesn't somebody go after that giant? If no one else will, I will"—and by God's grace he brought Goliath down with a strong faith and one smooth stone. Nehemiah heard that the walls of Jerusalem had fallen into disrepair, so he wept and fasted and prayed. He couldn't be satisfied to leave things like that. He inspected the walls, gathered the people together and said, "Let's rise up and build!" Jesus didn't just whine about spiritual mismanagement in the temple; he took action, cast out the moneychangers, and said, "My house will be called a house of prayer" (Matthew 21:13).

Marcus Buckingham has said, "You are a leader if, and only if, you are restless for change, impatient for progress, and deeply dissatisfied with the status quo. As a leader, you are never satisfied with the present, because in your head you can see a better future, and the friction between 'what is' and 'what could be' burns you up, stirs you up, propels you forward."

This principle is basically the same whether you are the senior minister of a church, an NFL coach, a husband and wife trying to revitalize your marriage, or a boss trying to improve your business. Things won't change for the better until you get tired of the way things are. Leaders are in the transformation business, not the status quo keeping business. So is the Lord. Remember, he's the expert at making things new.

A New You

The word *new* has different meanings depending on the context. If you buy a used car with 100,000 miles on the odometer, you might call it your "new car." It's not fresh off the assembly line, but it's new to your driveway. What Alexander Graham Bell called his "new" telephone was quite unsophisticated compared to the new smartphone you carry in your pocket.

In biblical times there were different Greek words for new. *Neos* meant new in terms of time; if something was new in this sense, it was recent or young. *Kainos* meant new in quality or form—in its very nature fresh or different from what is old. Some of us still use old-fashioned snail mail. We take a piece of paper, place it in an envelope, put a stamp on it, and drop it in a mailbox. When we started using e-mail, though, it was *kainos*—a whole new kind of mail—a new way to communicate.

Kainos (new in quality, not just in time) is the word used in 2 Corinthians 5:17, which says God makes us new creations in Christ. *Kainos* is the word for the new covenant Jesus died to establish (Hebrews 8:13), the new song that surrounds the throne of God (Revelation 5:9), and the new heaven and new earth awaiting God's people (Revelation 21:1). These blessings are not just new in terms of time; they are a huge leap forward in terms of quality.

After Jesus died, Joseph of Arimathea and Nicodemus removed his body from the cross. John's Gospel says they placed his body in "a new tomb, in which no one had ever been laid" (John 19:41). The word John used for Jesus' "new" tomb was *kainos* (new in quality or form). Jesus' empty tomb introduced a new quality of hope to the world. His resurrection changes everything.

A friend of mine runs a company that rents space in a building in downtown Indianapolis. A jewelry manufacturer used to occupy the floor where his offices are now. (You can still see jeweler stations and a safe where the jewelry was kept.) When the jeweler left that space so another tenant could move in, the landlord pulled up the carpeting and sent it to a local cleaning firm. They flushed out $50K worth of gold dust from the carpeting from all the particles that had accumulated over the years. As it turns out, a dirty carpet that seemed to have no value was literally worth its weight in gold. The people in that office didn't realize that they were walking on gold dust every day.

Our own lives are a treasure, and so are the lives of those God entrusts to our leadership and guidance. In our own strength alone, you and I can't make ourselves new in terms of time, but the Lord can keep making us new in terms of quality. God is in the transformation business. Like a master jeweler, he can take the gold rings we call our lives, cut them apart, and make them more beautiful, fitting, and useful than ever before.

Application Questions

1. Consider that your ability to experience transformation is correlated to your relationship with the Lord. With that in mind, how would you describe your current potential? What needs to change in your relationship with God to enhance your growth potential?

2. In which of the following areas do you excel, and in which do you struggle? a) Mentoring, b) Spiritual renewal, c) Life-long learning, d) Perspective, e) Calling. How do those realities impact your transformation efforts?

3. Which brings you greater fulfillment—preaching an effective sermon or listening to an effective sermon preached by someone you mentored? Why?

4. What are some of the nagging forms of discontentment that drive you to pursue transformation?

5. Look into the future a year or two. Describe the "new you" that you want to be. In what specific ways is that person different from the one you looked at in the mirror this morning?

Group Discussion Questions

1. Recount your experiences of having to take apart a complex toy, appliance, or tool. How easy was it to put back together? Did you run into any problems? What was the end result of your "repair?" What did you learn from the experience?

2. Consider 1 Timothy 4:12. What insecurities are you allowing to hinder your transformation efforts? What productive activities are you avoiding, relationships are you dodging, and words are you muting as a result of those insecurities?

3. Why is perseverance critical in order to achieve ongoing transformation? Describe an occasion or experience in which you gave up on a goal after you exerted a lot of time and effort. What would you do differently if you had the opportunity to go back and try again?

4. What older person are you connected with in a transparent relationship? Who are you being transparent with that is younger than you? What do you bring to the table in those relationships? What unique things do you gain from each relationship?

5. What five things can you do, stop doing, or do differently in order to better leverage transparency in your attempts to achieve transformation?

TRANSFORMATION
through ACCOUNTABILITY

ALAN AHLGRIM

CHAPTER 8

GOD'S LOVE THAT ALLOWS ACCOUNTABILITY

I hate accountability! Okay, so most people do, but then most people haven't been asked to write a chapter encouraging and affirming its value for Christian leaders. Don't misunderstand, I believe accountability to be of great value and even essential for true transformation. I just don't believe that accountability can be forced. After decades of leading local churches I came to realize that no one will ever be any more accountable than he or she wants to be! You can't make me do what I don't want to do, at least not for long or with a decent attitude. Even if I agree to be a good soldier and follow the rules, that doesn't mean my heart will be in it or that I am being truthful about it.

Sometimes we're all tempted to put on a false face and pretend to be what we're not. For years I required all staff members to turn in weekly reports that detailed the amount of time invested in ministry, and also to share the major investments of their day, week or month. Sure enough, with heavy duty reminders most of the dozens on our staff would reluctantly (and often belatedly) submit the required report. These reports had the potential of being highly valuable, both for communication and also for encouragement. But most of the staff seemed to consider them a mere busy work intrusion and worse, an interruption of their high and important calling. One of our young interns was in the habit of submitting reports with scant information. He even used a squiggly line and scribbled "contact time" over huge segments of the calendar he submitted to his supervisor. Only much later did we come to realize just what "contact time" really meant. That happened when he was criminally charged with illicit sexual contact with many of the underage boys he was supposed to be mentoring.

Accountability can't be forced. Now, go back to check out the title of this chapter and you'll see that a heavy handed accountability is not what we're talking about. The appeal is for voluntary accountability rooted in a relationship of trust and truthfulness. While we're daily reminded of the failures of our national leaders to be honorable and truthful, we're also painfully and frequently reminded of the failures of church leaders to be godly. We all know better; why then don't we do better, when most of us yearn to be holy? Well, as has been said, "Christian leaders don't fall because they forget they are holy; they fall because they forget they are human."

ACCOUNTABILITY ONLY HAPPENS INTENTIONALLY!

Our humanity requires us to practice intentional accountability! My struggles, both recent and long ago, regularly remind me of my own humanity. I can still vividly recall a tempting situation from decades ago — maybe I was attracted to this cute little brunette because she looked a lot like my own wife! Anyway, when she set up a counseling appointment with me, I felt my heart beat faster and it really scared me. Just before she came in I called a minister friend and asked him to pray for me...and fast! At first he laughed as if I was just joking around, but when he realized how serious I was, he stopped laughing. The good news is that through my confession and his intercession I successfully endured that temptation. The bad news is when my friend later faced a similar temptation, he didn't make a similar call to me or to anyone else. His actions ended up destroying both his marriage and his ministry.

None of us is as strong as we wish we were. That's why over 20 years ago I began talking weekly and meeting regularly with a psychologist friend, Dr. John Walker. I recently uncovered the questions that we invited each other to ask. I won't share John's, but here are mine.

Questions for Alan on every F.A.C.E.T.

1. *Are you Focusing on Linda or fantasizing?*
2. *Are you Accepting others?*

3. *Are you **C**hoosing to do things or obsessing on "should's"?*
4. *Are you **E**njoying a sabbath and having fun?*
5. *Are you **T**rusting that God knows your name? (Isaiah 43:1)*

John knew my insecurities well. That's why he regularly emphasized that God's grace wasn't just for others. It was for me! I needed that reminder. I didn't want or need "accountability" as much as I wanted and needed acceptance and encouragement. How about you? For most of us, asking for accountability almost sounds like inviting someone to snoop around in our dirty laundry or catch us doing something wrong. More than anything, what we all need is for someone we love and trust to come along side of us and catch us doing something right! We thrive on being understood and encouraged.

John and I are no longer "accountability partners." That morphed into what he called "intentional collegiality." Leave it to a Ph.D. psychologist to come up with a term like that! What it boils down to is that we came alongside each other in support and encouragement, not in correction or blame. A true friend knows and loves us well enough to speak truth to us. Affirming truth. Clarifying truth. Hard truth.

A few years ago I was on the brink of making a big mistake. At a time of great weariness of body and soul I was ready to suddenly resign. I was even composing the letter in my head as I walked my dog in the dark of the night. The next morning when I told my friend about that, his tone suddenly shifted from support to challenge. He said, "Whatever you do, don't do that! In fact, before you do anything so radical it's imperative that you talk with two people, first, to your wife and then to one other person you trust. That person doesn't have to be me, but if it is me, then listen now - you must not do anything so life altering without processing it with me first. Do you understand?!"

John's strong words worked. Why? That was just the sort of challenge and "accountability" that I needed because it was rooted in a long term relationship of love and trust. I listened to him and heeded him because I knew that John only wanted the best for me and my ministry. That's why I agreed to be "accountable" by not doing anything consequential without first consulting with him. I will be forever grateful that I did.

Every Christian needs accountability, and every Christian leader needs it even more! In the early days of the Wesleyan movement, believers were clustered together in small groups that met weekly. Every week each group member was asked, "How is it with your soul?" After that, a number of other probing questions followed.

Sadly, Christian leaders these days are far more likely to be challenged to focus on "strategic planning" rather than on "strategic reflection." Yet seldom does a church leader go off the rails because a ministry initiative, sermon series or growth goal isn't reached. Instead, virtually every case of an embarrassing or awkward leadership transition is due to a character or relational failure. While we will never be able to prevent all ministry meltdowns, we can do more to minimize the number of them. It all begins with a clear commitment to intentionality in our individual accountability.

I was challenged many years ago to begin building an intercessory prayer team. I was shocked by how easy that was. I simply approached a few trusted folks who had repeatedly told me that they faithfully (even daily!) prayed for me. When someone agreed to serve me by praying for me, I then asked if they would like to receive a monthly update from me. You won't be surprised that they all immediately said they would be honored by that and highly interested in receiving it. After hearing that, I was highly motivated to produce it! That's what started my discipline of intentional accountability. I've now used the same format for decades and it's been catalytic in keeping me on track with my calling.

Every update follows the same Review-Analysis-Plan (R.A.P.) format. I begin with a review of the high points since my last update. That practice never ceases to amaze me. Even when I don't feel like I've accomplished very much, by the time I finish listing many of the consequential things that I have done or that have happened, I'm always encouraged. Then I share a paragraph or two of analysis, attempting to share some key learnings and feelings. Finally, I list some of the major items or events coming up that are of special note and close with a few of the favorite insights and quotes I have recently gleaned.

Leaders all live in the land of the urgent. Recruiting a team of intercessors and faithfully communicating with them is not urgent, but when it comes to personal accountability few things may be as important! How many ministries could be sharpened, strengthened or even saved if every minister determined to follow this simple pattern of "strategic reflection?" I've been making this point for decades, and even sharing my own R.A.P.'s widely, but to my knowledge rarely do many other leaders actually determine to implement this in their own ministry. Why? While many affirm the potential value of practicing this sort of personal discipline they really don't want to be that "accountable."

Those in public roles often have private struggles with personal disciplines. Truth be told, we avoid disclosure and prefer to guard our privacy. We don't want to pull back the curtain and let too many people see too much. While we shouldn't share our intimate secrets in a prayer letter, and while we can't divulge confidentialities of the ministry, we can and should alert a trusted team of leaders and intercessors to the highs and lows of our life and leadership. This is not only good for those we're in partnership with, it's good for our own soul. As King David said, "I pondered the direction of my life, and turned to follow your laws" (Psalm 119:59; NLT). And as the apostle Paul said to Timothy, "Reflect on what I am saying, for the Lord will give you insight into all this...." (2 Timothy 2:7).

Pondering the past and the discipline of reflection are key to moving forward. In a fast paced and frenetic culture we all need to daily press pause to reflect on God's Word and what He is saying to us. The simple discipline of beginning my morning reading of Scripture with the chapter of Proverbs corresponding to the day's date, not to mention a Psalm or several, has not only kept me out of the ditch but emboldened me for leadership. This is beyond important for me. This is essential. Sadly, most Christians and even many Christian leaders have yet to learn this delightful and soul enriching discipline.

Most leaders are drug addicts. Recent brain research documents that the constant bombardment of email, text messages, Facebook, Instagram and other social media is highly addictive. We actually get an immediate dopamine hit when we receive an alert via social media. Even when there is apparently no time for the discipline of reflection, there is always time for social media. Unfortunately, there's a reason why drugs are called "dope" ... they make us dopey!

While we all know we grow best through times of retreat and reflection, we end up trading the pleasure of a short term fix for the fulfillment of a long term reward. Only through personal discipline do many leaders discover the value of beginning their day slowly and quietly. This sort of discipline is not an easy one to implement for anyone, that's why it requires some sort of intentional accountability.

I recently heard of two young associate ministers that agreed to hold each other accountable to begin their mornings with their Bibles open and their technology off. Several years ago the founder of the International Justice Mission, Gary Haugen, a human rights attorney, decreed that his entire staff was to begin their work day with 30 minutes of reflection and prayer, free from any technology. Might this sort of intentionality be a key to their transformational results?

ACCOUNTABILITY HAPPENS OVER TIME!

Spiritual growth, as with physical growth, takes time. In M. Robert Mulholland's classic book, *Invitation to a Journey - A Road Map for Spiritual Transformation,* I found this insightful definition: "Spiritual formation is a process of being formed in the image of Christ for the sake of others." In other words, growth doesn't happen overnight, it only happens over time. It takes time to mature. Humility for example, isn't automatic. For many of us, humility is the sort of character quality that always seems out of reach. Just when I think I'm being humble I often find myself recognizing it, and worse, even taking pride in it. Ugh!

How humble are you? Edward Benson became archbishop of Canterbury in 1882 and suggested a few "humble" rules for Christian leaders and others:

- *Do not murmur at your busyness or the shortness of the time.*

- *Never exaggerate duties by seeming to suffer under the load.*

- *Never call attention to crowded work or trivial experiences.*

- *Before confrontation or censure, obtain from God a real love for the one at fault.*

- *Do not believe everything you hear; do not spread gossip.*

- *Do not seek praise, gratitude, respect, or regard for past service.*

- *Avoid complaining when your advice or opinion is not consulted, or having been consulted, set aside.*

- *Never allow yourself to be placed in favorable contrast with anyone.*

- *Seek no favors, nor sympathies; do not ask for tenderness, but receive what comes.*

Humility is hard because it actually requires both self-awareness and self-denial. I find it helpful to review a list like the one above and acknowledge how often my pride is at play and gets in the way. As the saying goes, *it's not about thinking less of yourself, but rather thinking about yourself less.* According to Jesus this is pretty important. "For all those who exalt themselves will be humbled, and those who humble themselves will be exalted" (Luke 14:11).

Every Christian leader should specialize in the practice *of truth and not just the* proclamation *of it.* We often tell others the importance of daily reading and reflection in the Word . . . weekly worship and rest . . . faithfulness in tithing plus generosity beyond . . . frequent soul-enriching connections and consistent exercise for good stewardship of the body. Yet all too often we fail to consistently do all, or even half, of those things ourselves.

How would you rate yourself on each of the above? The reality is that few leaders are consistently practicing what they preach. We don't always eat our own cooking! The question is "Why?"

As I processed this with Dr. John Walker, he raised the pervasive problem of arrogance *among leaders.* Yes, arrogance. We tend to see ourselves as special. All too often we firmly believe that while others may need these disciplines, we do not. John even referenced something he heard me say a few years ago. I was talking about King Solomon. The king's problem was not in seeing himself as exceptional; his problem was in seeing himself as the exception! King David said, "Keep me from lying to myself; give me the privilege of knowing your instructions" (Psalm 119:29). Our arrogance is our undoing. It's not just the isolated leader that is the vulnerable leader;

the arrogant leader is the vulnerable leader. As I shared this with one of my Fraternity Covenant Groups, everyone resonated. One of the guys talked about how this is illustrated by the arrogant Pharisee who prayed: "God, I thank you that I am not like other people" (Luke 18:11).

The reality is that we are all prone to self-deception, and we all have blind spots. It seems that famous people can be especially famous for this. As the son of actor Robert Redford said, "My father, like everyone else, had a capacity for self-absolving denial." The only way for light to shine at times is through candid, confidential conversation in safe settings.

The Lily Endowment gave out 84 million dollars through their Sustaining Pastoral Excellence *program*. This made it possible for more than 60 different organizations to study what enabled pastors to serve well and finish well. The one thing most all groups agreed upon was that pastors need peer groups... preferably from other networks and denominations. Pastors are people too; therefore, pastors are by nature competitive and fearful. That's why we need to share our stuff with those to whom we do not report and those who do not report to us. Psychologists talk about the danger and difficulty of "dual role relationships" among Christian leaders. That is, for a pastor and chairman of the elders to expect to enjoy a fully disclosing friendship is expecting too much. The same is true for a youth minister with a lead minister, or a church planter with a church planting executive. Dual role relationships are problematic and can unintentionally lead to feelings of isolation and even desperation.

Everyone needs to be able to share their challenges and process their struggles in safe settings. That's when light shines the brightest. It's only then and there that many of us will ever determine to consistently do what we are telling others to do! David Benner has written a profound book entitled, *Sacred Companions: The Gift of Spiritual Friendship and Direction.* He says, "The hunger for connection is one of the most fundamental desires of the human heart.... In the core of our being we yearn for intimacy. We want people to share our lives. We want soul friends.... Paradoxically, however, what we most deeply long for we also fear."[35]

Benner calls these special allies "sacred companions" or "spiritual

---

35. David Benner, *Sacred Companions: The Gift of Spiritual Friendship and Direction* (Downers Grove, IL: InterVarsity Press, 2002), p. 14.

friends." He says, "If you are making significant progress on the transformational journey of Christian spirituality, you have one or more friendships that support that journey. If you do not, you are not. It's that simple."

So, who are the sacred allies in your soul care fraternity? Here are seven clues to help you identify them:

- Who breathes life into you rather than sucks life out of you?
- Who challenges you spiritually?
- Who sharpens you mentally?
- Who is a friend of your excitement?
- Who makes you laugh?
- Who can keep a confidence?
- Who leaves you feeling more alive?

Great leaders have great friends. I'm struck by the affirming words of the apostle Paul about his young friend Timothy. "I have no one else of kindred spirit who will genuinely be concerned for your welfare." Paul endorsed one friend to another. One of the gifts that we give to each other is the gift of introductions. I love to introduce my friends to others, and I love it when others introduce their friends to me. Might your life be just one call or email away from being better? Yes, of course! There's no better time than now to take some relational initiative. So, which ally might be ready and willing to enrich you and to be enriched by you?

Some Christian leaders have big heads and small hearts. "Shop talk" can be a good thing, but it's merely a "heady" thing to focus primarily on ideas, information and inspiration. By contrast, "soul care" is more of a heart thing, especially focusing on insight, illumination and transformation. There are three essential ingredients in the recipe for transformational covenant groups:

- *Courageous candor must be led:* ". . . only he who is able to articulate his own experience can offer himself to others as a source of clarification. The Christian leader is, therefore, first of all, a man who is willing to put his own articulated faith at the disposal of those who ask for his help. In this sense he is a servant of servants, because he is the first to enter the promised but dangerous land, the first to tell those who are afraid what he has seen, heard and touched."[36]

- *Humble vulnerability must be modeled:* "The way of trust is a movement into obscurity, into the undefined, into ambiguity, not into some pre-determined clearly delineated plan for the future . . . the reality of naked trust is the life of the pilgrim who leaves what is nailed down, obvious, and secure, and walks into the unknown without any rational explanation to justify the decision or guarantee the future. Why? Because God has signaled the movement and offered it His presence and His promise."[37]

- *Deep non-judgmental listening is a must to build trust:* "Listening is a magnetic and strange thing, a creative force. The friends who listen to us are the ones we move toward. When we are listened to, it creates us, makes us unfold and expand." Dr. Karl Menninger

Leaders crave community, but rarely experience it. This kind of experience must be intentionally led, sincerely embraced and fiercely guarded. The "Fraternity Covenant Group" model involves a strong commitment from five leaders to meet together twice each year and to connect monthly by conference calls over a course of three years. We believe that transformational soul care is a journey, not a destination; and we encourage all Christian leaders to pursue it vigorously and joyfully . . . and from the heart.

It is rare for leaders to disclose their deepest feelings. Most desperately try to conceal their true heart condition for fear of what might happen. We all have a few things that few others will ever know, or even should know. Here are some "secrets" I've recently heard.

1. *"I'm not sure how much longer I want to do this."* Leading anything is hard, leading a local church is exhausting. As Dr. John Walker likes to remind pastors, "Nothing requires more of you than ministry." Being "on" and available and prepared at all times is impossible. That's one reason why the vast majority of those who begin in ministry don't

---

36. Henri Nouwen, *The Wounded Healer: Ministry in Contemporary Society* (New York: Doubleday, 1979), p. 38.
37. Brennan Manning, *Ruthless Trust: The Ragamuffin's Path to God* (New York: HarperCollins, 2000), pp. 12-13.

actually finish in ministry. While not everyone flames out in some flagrant fashion, many just lose their capacity or desire to go on.

2. *"I'm shocked by how sin still stalks me!"* Whether the struggle is with lust, pornography, alcohol or anger, everyone faces the unrelenting reminder of their humanity. While we can all easily admit to faults in a general sense, or with a carefully crafted illustration from a time long ago and in a place far away, the reality is that our struggles are not all minor ones or all rooted in ancient history. All too often our struggles and sins are current events... we just can't admit them in real time for fear others will lose confidence in us. We're not sure who we can trust with our stuff.

3. *"I'm waking every morning with thoughts of failure."* There's never been a time when the stakes were so high and the expectations so unrealistic. This is especially true in the local church. No minister could hope to fulfill even 80% of the hopes and dreams of those in any given congregation. Not a week goes by that a leader isn't reminded by someone that he just doesn't measure up in some way. Some of that may be legitimate; however, many criticisms are petty, pointless and even ridiculous. Here's the ugly truth, the greatest critic of most every leader is the one he sees in the mirror every morning.

4. *"I'm increasingly feeling out of touch and irrelevant."* The times are changing for sure! While not long ago leaders in their 50's and even 60's were considered to be in their leadership prime, now they're the "old guys." As churches consider candidates to be their next "senior leader" he is unlikely to be very "senior," or even much over the age of 40. One large congregation is seeking a gifted preacher between 28-33 to lead them in a high growth area. While many strong leaders and communicators can certainly be found in that age bracket, few would honestly describe themselves as mature, experienced or seasoned leaders. Yet those are the leaders most in demand right now.

5. *"I'm feeling unappreciated."* One pastor told me that he hates "Pastor Appreciation Month," the celebration promoted each October on Christian radio. This minister hates it, not because he

hates appreciation but because he needs it and rarely receives it. That hurts. What can hurt even more is when the pastor's wife is rarely recognized for the contribution and sacrifices she makes for the good of the church. It's painful to be repeatedly taken for granted simply because you're called to be a servant leader.

6. *"I'm feeling misunderstood."* Every leader lives with pressure and private pain at times. That's especially true for those in high stress roles. Who better understands what it's like to be a surgeon, with someone's life literally in your hands, than another surgeon? Who better understands what it's like to be a cop called to defuse a domestic violence situation than another cop? And who better understands what it's like to be a minister using the Bible to address controversial issues in public such as sexual abstinence or gay marriage than another pastor? In addition to preaching weekly on a wide variety of topics, the typical minister gets dizzy changing hats for the wide variety of other roles he is expected to fill. To be a leader is to be both stretched and misunderstood.

The not so secret "secret" is that church leaders live with stress that eats away at their confidence and joy. However, once these stresses are expressed and addressed they become less formidable and more manageable. No leader is ever truly alone in what he faces or how he feels. Isolation is just the devil's tool to discourage and dishearten those in vital roles, and the isolated leader is the most vulnerable leader. The reality is that everyone can relate to stress; however, properly understood it can remind us of the ultimate solution.

Jesus is the ultimate leader. Jesus knew stress. He knew temptation, disappointment, criticism, abandonment and betrayal. If anyone can understand what a leader must endure, Jesus can. That's why Jesus has the credibility to counsel us. Jesus said, "Here's what I want you to do: Find a quiet secluded place so you won't be tempted to role-play before God. Just be there as simply and honestly as you can manage. The focus will shift from you to God, and you will begin to sense his grace" (Matthew 6: 5-8, The Message).

Here's how healthy accountability is experienced in a Fraternity Covenant Group context.

- *We wrench the time out of our crazy calendars.* We talk by phone monthly and meet face-to- face twice a year. These gatherings are rarely convenient, but they are consistently invigorating. Rarely does anyone ever miss one of these in-depth opportunities that we've scheduled.

- *We share unguardedly.* While each of us leads a public life, these gatherings are highly personal, versus pastoral and professional. No one feels that he has to be "on" or "measured" in what he says or how he says it. That's why we can share our stresses and struggles without fear of judgment. Refreshing candor is the standard.

- *We waste very little time talking shop.* We spend most of our time doing the hard work of heart work. As C.S. Lewis said, "Lovers bare their bodies, friends bare their souls." Confidentiality is one of the keys to candor. That's why it's not uncommon to hear someone say, "I've never told anyone this before."

- *We have no agenda for each other.* Christian leaders live in the land of agendas. We always have things we want others to do in the church, and many church people more than return the favor of expressing their agendas for us! In these gatherings we're not trying to fix, motivate, inspire, challenge or lead each other. We give each other the liberating gift of acceptance. As my buddy Cam Huxford once said, "Refreshing friends don't try to change you, rather they make you want to change."

- *We listen hard.* We sometimes take notes on what is said and even probe for deeper reflection. As we relax together we grow together. These free-flowing, yet intentional conversations, often lead to light-shining discoveries and sometimes even to tears. Good friends ask good questions that help us to explore and grow, even through pain.

Most people rarely, if ever, get to this level of trust, especially Christian leaders... in part because it takes time. While we're the ones who talk and teach the most about community, we often enjoy it the least. That's because life is moving too fast. However, life change doesn't happen at the speed of light but at the slow speed of love. Lingering conversations are essential for relational fulfillment and life transformation.

Jesus was the ultimate relational investor. No one had a more important assignment than He did, yet Jesus invested in-depth time with His disciples. He made it clear that He first called each of them to simply be with Him. Then in John 15 He said, *"… I have called you friends, for everything that I have learned from my Father I have made known to you … I chose you and appointed you to go and bear fruit that will last."*

Relationships are the only thing that will last; they're the only thing we take to heaven with us. Who are the ones who know you the best and accept you the most? Might it be that some of the richest relationships you've ever had are still yet ahead? I hope so. Even though I'm already relationally mega-wealthy, I'm still heavily investing…expecting and experiencing wonderful returns. How about you? Someone said, "Become an accepting person, and you will have a long line of people at your door!" Everyone longs for acceptance. It's true of middle school kids, mega-church pastors and even muscle-bound NFL linemen. There are no exceptions when it comes to the drive for acceptance. I have been an acceptance addict and I've paid a high price. The desire for acceptance has at times driven me to ridiculous levels of performance in people pleasing and approval seeking. I didn't want to disappoint anyone. I wanted everyone to be happy with me and admire my efforts to serve them and others. I even sacrificed my family, free time and health in the service of others. While not everything I've done in ministry has been self-serving; neither has it always been completely noble and self-denying.

Love is acceptance. For reasons I can't fully explain, I was prompted to paraphrase this familiar passage on love by simply inserting the word *accept, accepted* or *acceptance* every time love was referenced. The text went from black words on a white page to words leaping off the page highlighted by the Holy Spirit. Here it is from I John 4:7-12.

"Dear friends, let us continue to <u>accept</u> one another, for <u>acceptance</u> comes from God. Anyone who <u>accepts</u> is a child of God and knows God. But anyone who does not <u>accept</u> does not know God, for God is <u>acceptance</u>. God showed how much he <u>accepted</u> us by sending his one and only Son into the world so that we might have eternal life through him. This is real <u>acceptance</u> – not that we <u>accepted</u> God, but that he <u>accepted</u> us and sent his Son as a sacrifice to take away our sins. Dear friends, since God <u>accepted</u> us that much, we surely ought to <u>accept</u> each other. No one has ever seen God. But if we <u>accept</u> each other, God lives in us, and his <u>acceptance</u> is brought to full expression in us."

I dare you to read that passage again using the acceptance words and sharing them out loud with a trusted friend. I've heard it said that no one ever changes unless someone accepts him first! Acceptance is the gift God gives us through Jesus, and acceptance is the gift we give to others through his grace. Here are the steps:

- Accept that you are totally accepted by God's grace.

- Celebrate the gift of God's acceptance by admitting your desperate need for it.

- Accept the imperfections of others close to you, just as you would like them to accept yours.

I've been addicted to receiving acceptance…now, by God's grace I'm becoming devoted to *extending* acceptance. That doesn't merely happen in theory, it only really happens in community!

Application Questions

1. Are ministers, and you specifically, more or less likely to wear "masks" than the average person in the congregation? Why or why not?

2. Which of the following thoughts do you struggle with most often? a) I'm not sure how much longer I want to do this, b) I'm shocked by how sin still stalks me, c) I'm waking every morning with thoughts of failure, d) I'm increasingly feeling out of touch and irrelevant, e) I'm feeling unappreciated, f) I'm feeling misunderstood. In what ways could a strategic relationship help you overcome that struggle?

3. Who are your three best friends? Which friend is best suited to ask you probing questions? How often do you invite that person – or someone else – to speak hard truths into your life and/or ministry?

4. What is the biggest mistake you almost made but avoided as a result of someone else talking you out of it? What is the biggest mistake that you talked someone else out of making?

5. On a scale of 1 (not at all) to 10 (totally), to what degree do feel accepted by the following people? a) God, b) your family, c) your peers, d) your congregants. How do those scores affect the way you approach relationships?

Group Discussion Questions

1. Which of the following insecurities do you struggle with most? a) Your body shape, b) The way you talk, c) The way you dress, d) Your friends, e) Your education, f) Your income, g) Your career, h) Your perceived value, i) Other (please specify). In what ways could strategic relationships help you overcome that insecurity?

2. How can social media help you pursue transformation? How can social media undermine your pursuit of transformation? Is the way you currently use social media helping or hurting your growth? In what specific ways does your use of social media need to change?

3. Are you more or less likely to perform a task if someone is pressuring you to do it? Why? Share an example of a time that you refused to do something – or stalled – simply because you didn't like the fact that someone was pushing you to complete the task.

4. Which of the following disciplines do you find most useful for producing transformation in your life? a) Prayer, b) Personal Bible study, c) Journaling, d) Serving e) Silence & solitude, f) Personal worship. How often do you practice that discipline? Set a goal for increasing your consistency in that discipline.

5. On a scale of 1 (not at all) to 10 (extremely), how humble would people closest to you say you are? In what ways does your humility score affect your ability to speak truth to others and receive truth being spoken to you?

CHAPTER 9

RELATIONSHIPS THAT ALLOW ACCOUNTABILITY

ACCOUNTABILITY HAPPENS IN COMMUNITY!

I don't want to hold others accountable so much as to hold them close. Here are questions I currently ask and answer monthly with a couple dozen ministers and Christian leaders over lunch, on the phone or in a small group setting. These questions are highly portable, they work anywhere:

1. *What is delighting you?*
2. *What is draining you?*
3. *What are you discovering?*

At times we also craft other "tough love" questions as well that are customized for each individual. None are asked with a spirit of condemnation, but rather out of compassion and concern. It's amazing how open I've found tough men to be when they feel understood, accepted and encouraged. In fact, the more we share our struggles, the more we grow to trust that we're not alone. We really feel like brothers. It's been said, "The more we share our successes, the more likely we are to be competitors; but the more we share our struggles, the more likely we are to become brothers."

Ministry is messy, but it doesn't have to be lonely. Sadly, most Christian leaders are seriously lonely at a soul level. While they enjoy many connections, they have very few heart level companions. In a recent survey of lead pastors, less than half felt that they could share their struggles with the elders of the church. Frankly, I'm surprised that nearly half of ministers actually said that they could or would share their struggles and feelings candidly with the elders. From my experience of mentoring pastors, most have learned the hard way to be very cautious with those who not only set their salaries, but who hold their future in their hands.

Here are a few questions for you to ponder:

1. Who are you close to? The isolated person is the vulnerable person!

2. Where are you most vulnerable right now? You're only as sick as your secrets!

3. What are the questions you most need to be asked? You'll only be as open as you choose to be!

Are you committed to staying close to others in a consistent, meaningful and authentic way? Let's face it …all relationships aren't created equal, nor do they all carry the same level of responsibility for disclosure. Here's how I have pictured and presented the three levels of responsible connection that we all need to have.

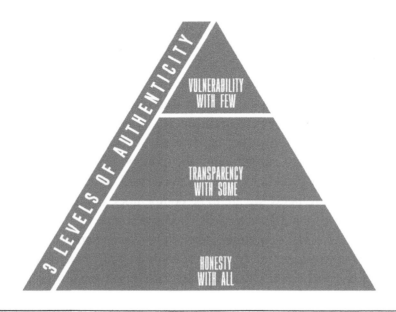

Note that there is always to be authenticity at all three levels. It's just that being a truth teller doesn't mean that everyone has the right to know everything that others know. For example, while we tell the truth to those we are selling a car or house to, we're not under obligation to share the struggles of our health and home life. Those sorts of things are reserved for a small number of trusted friends and allies such as the team we work with or the small group we fellowship with. However, when it comes to baring our soul and talking about our greatest fears, our deepest hurts and our most embarrassing failures, that level of vulnerability should be shared only with great caution and discretion, and with a select few. Most staff, elder and leadership teams never move beyond the second level of authenticity, that of transparency, nor should they. The top level of vulnerability is rare air indeed, but it is vital that we breathe that air with a trusted few. That's because the isolated person is the vulnerable person… in this case, vulnerable to defeat!

Everyone needs authentic connections. Those relationship connections come in all shapes and sizes and levels. While all relationships should be rooted in honesty, only some mature to the level of transparency with a trusted few. The capacity for transparency is the foundation for true vulnerability. Without the risk of vulnerability we will never enjoy true loyalty. With whom are you vulnerable? When you answer that question I will tell you where you will enjoy your greatest rewards. As psychiatrist and author Scott Peck has observed, "There can be no vulnerability without risk. There can be no community without vulnerability. There can be no peace – and ultimately no life – without community."

Friendship isn't cheap. There's a cost to true community. Quality connections can't happen without consistent interaction and investment. It not only takes time to know another and to be known by another – it takes vulnerability. Gordon MacDonald shares a story about a rabbi sitting in his study when his reading was interrupted by a knock on the door. It was one of his students who simply wanted to tell him how much he loved him. The rabbi put down his book and looked over his glasses and asked, "What hurts me?" The student was confused, so the rabbi asked him again, "What hurts me?" The boy was speechless at first and finally responded, "I don't know." To which the wise rabbi said, "How can you love me if you don't know what hurts me?"

It's fascinating to me that while everyone craves deep connection and longs for true community, very few enjoy it – even Christian leaders. I recently had a conversation with a young leader with significant national influence who admitted to me that he had no close friends. While he has several men that he respects and trusts, he admits that he hasn't really made the investment necessary to move to the next level and become truly close to them. That's not at all uncommon.

Another leader of a large church once told me that he always struggled with the impostor syndrome. He fears that if others knew, especially other leaders, just how hard it is for him to read, that he would be exposed as inadequate and they would look down on him. As a result, he often avoided opening up to other leaders and getting close to them, much less becoming vulnerable with them.

We all struggle with relationships at times. While they are the source of our greatest fulfillment, they are also the source of our greatest frustrations, failures and grief. Relationships are unpredictable and risky. Yet, we were all created to have and enjoy them. The best relationships happen when vulnerability is embraced. However, the greatest fear of many is that being vulnerable will lead to being judged or rejected. What would you do or say if you weren't afraid? A few years ago I took the high-risk conversation of addressing a challenging issue with a close friend. I was totally vulnerable as I shared my heart-felt concern for his life situation. I passionately shared a pointed challenge that could have destroyed our relationship; instead it deepened it!

The Trinity is the model of perfect community. Just as the Father, Son and Holy Spirit enjoy an open relationship with nothing held back, the same is to be true of us. My closest friends tell me embarrassing things, and I do the same with them. We don't just tell each other things we're proud of, but also things we're struggling with. It's a funny thing how the very sharing of our failures, foibles, and fears always ends up drawing us closer together. That just happened again during a deep conversation over lunch. In the course of our time together, the four of us not only laughed a lot, we each opened up a lot. Each of us shared some of our junk, not because it was forced out of us but because there is trust between us.

As you evaluate the three levels of your trusted friendships, you might find these questions to be clarifying.

1. Do I consistently tell all the truth that's appropriate for the situation?

2. Do I disclose my insecurities as freely as I share my victories?

3. Do I have a trusted few that know what has hurt me and how I have hurt others?

We all long for deeper connections but that doesn't happen accidentally, it only happens intentionally through community. Jesus modeled just that. I find it more than fascinating that Jesus called us all to be in community, but that unlike most of us, Jesus actually lived this not just in the Trinity but when he called the twelve to be *with* him. The disciples did life with Jesus – they lived both the ordinary days with him and the extraordinary days. That's why he called them his friends.

Dallas Willard calls our success in making Christians and our failure in making disciples, "the great omission."[38] Jesus said: "A new command I give you, love one another as I have loved you, so you must love one another. By this all men will know that you are my disciples, if you love one another" (John 13:34-35).[39] The first focus of Jesus was not on building a crowd, but a community. Jesus wanted His disciples to be as committed to their community as he was. As church leaders, we're not doing so well with that these days. Most of us talk more about quantity than quality. We're far more concerned about the size of our church than the health of it. Health is measured more by the intangibles – things like honesty, transparency and vulnerability.

So, if you weren't afraid, what would you do and what would you say? There's no better time than now to begin moving in the direction of deeper connections. Ministry is hard but no one has to do ministry alone. By God's grace the opportunity to develop richer relationships is available to us all; in fact, some of your best relationships this side of heaven may be yet to be! How long has it been since you dared to share your heart and even took the risk of asking someone to illuminate your blind spots? The truth is,

---

38. Dallas Willard, *The Great Omission: Reclaiming Jesus's Essential Teachings on Discipleship* (New York: HarperCollins, 2006).
39. Scriptures referenced in this chapter cite the New International Version unless otherwise noted.

we're surrounded by people God is seeking to use to speak into our lives. It's always our choice whether or not we will choose to listen. In Proverbs 13:20, Solomon wrote, "Walk with the wise and become wise."

Wisdom is shouting for our attention, but all too often we are oblivious. While hearing loss is a common malady associated with aging, one of the marks of youth is often a resistance to listening to anyone but their peers. One of the marks of maturity is to listen well to those who are wiser. Recently, the mature leader of a large ministry asked for some insights on assisting his young staff. I suggested that he ask them to reflect on three verses and three probing questions that emerge from Proverbs 15.

- Verse 7: "The lips of the wise give good advice; the heart of a fool has none to give." Question: *What wise advice have you recently received?*

- Verse 22: "Plans go wrong for lack of advice; many advisers bring success." Question: *Who are your wise advisors?*

- Verse 31: "If you listen to constructive criticism, you will be at home among the wise." Question: *What constructive criticism have you recently listened to?*

Scientists who have studied leaders with humility note that they have the capacity for objective self-assessment. That is, they have an accurate view of themselves, one that's neither too high nor too low. Leaders are good listeners. King David said, "Keep me from lying to myself" (Psalm 119). The apostle Paul said, "… examine yourselves to see if your faith is genuine. Test yourselves" (2 Corinthians 13:5).

The wise are lifelong listeners and learners. C.S. Lewis once said: "The next best thing to being wise oneself is to live in a circle of those who are."[40] Healthy feedback is the breakfast of champions and the illuminator of blind spots! This I know, your life will be no richer than your relationships. That's God's plan. He has designed us for connection. From the very beginning of the Bible the Lord made that clear when He declared, *"It is not good for man to be alone."* I used to think that only applied to men and marriage.

---

40. C.S. Lewis, in *They Asked for a Paper: Papers and Addresses* (1962), p. 63.

Now I'm beginning to see that both men and women, those married and those not, were all created to be in community. We are all better together and that's nowhere more obvious to us than when we face the brutal and scary challenges of life and leadership.

I continue to be indebted to my mentors who have helped to enrich me, stretch me and enlighten me. One of my more recent mentors, Bob Shank, shared an especially illuminating concept called, "The Table of Influence." Picture a big table with four "chairs" representing four dimensions or types of influence that we all need in order to flourish: The Work chair, the Wisdom chair, the Wealth chair and the Woo chair. Let me explain.

"Who are the invited guests at your table?"

- The Work Chair - Those who sharpen you.

- The Wisdom Chair - Those who deepen you.

- The Wealth Chair - Those who resource you.

- The Woo Chair - Those who connect you. (Woo stands for "winning others over."

We are all immeasurably and immensely blessed relationally. No matter where we live, in this age of technological connectivity we are all able to locate almost anyone we know, or have ever known, almost instantly. However, while we live in an age of easy technological connection, all too often we personally experience personal disconnection. While many have hundreds of Facebook friends, most have few face-to-face personal friends. In fact, over 70% of men say that they have no close friends, and the percentage is even higher among Christian leaders.

We're overwhelmed with information but craving community. We were made for intimacy - it's the unrelenting hunger of our heart. We all seek to be known, understood and connected. Sadly, there are many valid reasons for relational caution. Too many have faced betrayal, abandonment and personal judgement. I've long been intrigued and sobered by the observation that even Jesus didn't trust everyone. "But Jesus didn't trust them, because he knew human nature. No one needed to tell him what mankind is really like" (John 2:24-25; NLT).

Sometimes it's hard to trust people, even Christian people. It's especially hard to trust people with your personal struggles when they are the same ones listening to your sermons and setting your salary. Christian leaders must set appropriate boundaries in what we share. We must learn that it's okay to have an unspoken thought! However, we all need others we can trust and turn to for enlightenment and enrichment.

The good news is: "His divine power has given us everything we need for life and godliness according to His glorious riches in Christ Jesus" (2 Peter 1:3). We are not alone - we are all amazingly well resourced. We are all relationally blessed. Yes, all of us. Just take a moment and see if you can identify two or three people who might easily fit in one of the four chairs. Surely you have some who sharpen you professionally, deepen you in matters of the heart, resource you with their assets and attitude or connect you with their network of allies. I've got an ever changing list for each, that's why once or twice a year I refresh my list of refreshing friends. By the way, these friends don't all literally sit around a table with me at the same time; in fact, they don't even all know one another. What they do know, or wouldn't be surprised to hear or hear again, is that they are on the list of my top relational assets.

In his book, Scary Close, Donald Miller says that "In the next few years we will become a conglomerate of the people we hang with."[41] Then he says, "90% of people's problems could be prevented if they'd choose healthier people to give their hearts to?"[42]

Relationships are not only the best part of life and leadership but all too often they are also the hardest. That's why the apostle Paul said, "Do all that you can to live in peace with everyone" (Romans 12:18). Let's face it, that's not easy. Sometimes we come to realize that certain people are toxic to our soul. You'll often know whether you've been with a relational asset or an antagonist by how you feel afterward. If someone is chronically critical, judgmental, demanding or demeaning, get a clue. That person is not an asset. By contrast if a person consistently leaves you feeling lighter and more enlightened, that's someone you ought to regularly find room for in your calendar.

Courage isn't neck up, it's heart up. Until we are willing to be transparent and even vulnerable with another person, we will not be able to experience

---

41. Donald Miller, *Scary Close: Dropping the Act and Finding True Intimacy* (Nasville: Nelson Books, 2014), p. 74.
42. Ibid., p. 76.

God's best. Not long ago, I heard that recent brain research shows that using feeling words creates connections. One of the key abilities of the most successful leaders in business is the capacity to know what they and others feel in the moment.

More courageous moments can happen for us all; however, heart work is hard work! I appreciate author John Slavel's words, "The greatest difficulty in conversion is to win the heart to God and the greatest difficulty after conversion is to keep the heart with God. Heart work is hard work indeed."[43] An essential factor in healthy community is in identifying what John Ortberg called a few "full-disclosure friendships."[44] In my new season of ministry I am no longer serving as "pastor in charge" but rather as a "pastor at large." Nearly every day I am engaged in the fulfilling role of helping those who are serving on the front lines of local church ministry. What I can report is that while most pastors are joyful in public they are struggling in private.

- They *are running scared – uncertain how long they will be relevant.*

- They are running on fumes – uncertain how long they can keep up the pace.

- They are running alone – uncertain if anyone can understand how they feel.

One of the most insightful books on community is entitled: The Search to Belong. Joseph Myers shares a study done back in the 1960's by Edward T. Hall about four spheres of belonging.[45]

- The Public Space: _____ 12 feet +
- The Social Space _____ 4 to 12 feet
- The Personal Space _____ 18 inches to 4 feet
- The Intimate Space _____ 0 to 18 inches

43. John Flavel, *Keeping the Heart* (Christian Heritage, 1848).
44. John Orberg, *Christianity Today,* "Higher Stakes Friendship: Five Rules that Allow Friends to be Real" (Feb. 2012). http://www.christianitytoday.com/pastors/2012/february-online-only/higherstakes.html. Accessed November 2017.
45. Joseph Myers, *The Search to Belong: Rethinking Intimacy, Community, and Small Groups* (Grand Rapids: Zondervan, 2003), p. 20.

Could this mean that belonging is multidimensional? Might people belong to us on different levels? Several times recently I've introduced this concept to leaders and watched the lights come on. Picture this as four concentric rings of a circle.

- *The Public Space is the outer ring.* We are connected with our community or region as in: "Colorado is Bronco Country!" All true orange and blue Bronco fans love to see others in Bronco gear. That's my public sphere.

- *The Social Space is the next ring.* Picture the church lobby on Sunday where we easily exchange warm greetings with folks we recognize even if we don't know them well or even by name. That's the social sphere.

- *The Personal Space is the ring near the center.* This is the close space shared in a small group or at a lunch table with a free flow of information and updates. That's the personal sphere.

- *The Intimate Space is at the center.* This is where the most in-depth stuff occurs and where the naked truth is shared. This is the rarest of all.

Most leaders celebrate a great connection on the first three levels or spheres but rarely all four. Even though the privilege of sharing the naked truth with another person is vital for our well-being, most leaders rarely if ever experience it. We long for in-depth connections, but we also fear them. We fear embarrassment, exposure and most of all, rejection. Yet it's when we share at the intimate level and reveal the naked truth about ourselves and our struggles that we discover true community.

Many years ago in a place, far, far away, I was under enormous stress. During a meeting with the church elders they sincerely commiserated with me over the multiple crises we were facing. Finally one said, "Alan, we're in this thing together." I'm sad to say that I didn't respond graciously. Out of deep worry and weariness I said, "Well guys, it's like we're in a great storm at sea. The wind is blowing, the waves are crashing and I'm getting hammered as I try to hang on for dear life in a tiny dinghy. Meanwhile you guys are all standing safely on the deck of the Queen Mary. You're all leaning over the rail and shouting, 'Hang in there, Alan, we're all in this thing together.' Well, we're in the same storm but we're not in the same boat!"

I deeply regret saying that, but I felt overwhelmed and alone. There's nothing worse than going through a great challenge and feeling that no one truly understands. Sometimes in a crisis our feelings can lead us astray. Sometimes in the midst of life's chaos, we can be guilty of the worst sort of stinkin' thinkin'! I know... I've been there.

Recently I shared that story when consulting with a minister in the Midwest. I was commiserating with him in his ordeal and shared how I once felt alone in the dinghy, assuming that he might feel the same. To my surprise he immediately disagreed. He said, "Actually I really feel like our elders are in the dinghy with me – they've been great!"

Later when I met privately with the elders, I shared his comment. They were deeply touched. It meant the world to them to know that the lead minister felt so supported. It was more than gratifying to me to see the strength of their partnership. I have no doubt that they will survive the storm with unity because they all know they're in the dinghy together.

One key to surviving a crisis is to know we're not alone. Sure, we know that God is with us, but we also like to know that someone else truly gets it. It's reassuring to know that another human being not only cares, but also resonates with us and understands. There's nothing more powerful.

Two questions:

- If you're facing a storm of some sort right now, who is in your dinghy with you?

- Do you have others in your life facing a personal storm confident that you are in the dinghy with them?

"If one part suffers, every part suffers with it...All of you together are Christ's body, and each of you is part of it" (1 Corinthians 12:26-27).

Every leader not only needs another leader, every leader also needs a cadre of confidants and spiritual allies. In a recent Fraternity Covenant Group gathering I once again heard this loud and clear. Here are just three heart-felt testimonies from leaders in the group:

- *"I've never experienced anything like this before!"*

- *"I've been looking for a group like this for 12 years!"*

- *"I wouldn't be where I am right now without what God did in me through this group one year ago!"*

Transformation only happens over time and in community. That's God's plan. There is no instant remedy for personal growth. We cannot become what God is calling us to be without a deep connection with God and without a vital few to partner with us. Great leaders need great relationships to finish well.

Every athlete, like every man and every leader, wants to finish well. We all want to go out at the top of our game. But how many John Elways will there ever be? You may remember that after three Super Bowl losses Elway received tons of criticism. Many assumed Elway's hopes of finishing well would never be realized. They were wrong. John Elway won back-to-back Super Bowl victories in 1997 and 1998.

Elway was voted MVP of Super Bowl XXXIII, which would prove to be the final game of his illustrious career. He was then inducted into the Pro Football Hall of Fame in 2004, his first year of eligibility. As a pro football player, Elway certainly finished well. Football careers, as with all careers, come and go—but the Kingdom of Christ is forever. Few, if any, finish a career with anything resembling a Super Bowl victory. That's not the ultimate standard of success. Those who finish with diminished physical strength but growing spiritual strength are still the most successful of all.

What does it mean to "finish well"? One my of mentors loves to ask that question. Bob Buford has had an immense influence on me over the years. Bob made his millions in the early days of cable TV and determined to invest his life serving pastors of large churches. His mentor was the famed business leader, Peter Drucker, who once said to him: "Bob, your fruit grows on other people's trees." In many ways that is true for every leader entering the final season of life.

Our lives have no meaning apart from how we bless others in community. Some will accomplish much and even enjoy great fame by writing books or leading major enterprises. Most of us will truly be known by only a few; however, that's where our greatest influence will always be.

My concern is that those who know me the best will be those who respect me the most. Success for me has little to do with the size of the ministries I've led or what I've accumulated. In my seventh decade, success to me really has to do with who and how I love.

What are the markers of finishing well for you? A few years ago my wife and I did something very interesting. We each took ten pieces of paper and wrote ten things that might define finishing well for us. When we compared our lists we each borrowed something from the other; however, our items were amazingly similar. Linda just had more references to enjoying our grandkids than I did. I still need to concentrate more on that one!

When I showed my scraps of paper to a friend over lunch, he decided to do the same thing. What would be on your list? Everyone needs something to live for . . . something that inspires them to look forward to the future. Personally, although I'm now 70 years old, most days I feel like I'm going on 50! I'm still energized because I still have important stuff to do. How about you?

Awhile back I was reviewing Bob Buford's book, Finishing Well. One of the amazing interviews he did was with the famed Bible teacher, Dr. Howard Hendricks. Bob asked Dr. Hendricks what the Bible had to say about finishing well. Hendricks reported an interesting study done by Fuller Seminary on about 100 people in the Bible who had enough data to study. Only about one third finished well. Most of them failed in the second half. Here's what he reported: "The thing that surfaced over and over was a failure, not in their knowledge of Scripture but in failing to apply Scripture in their lives. It was feeling that because they knew the Word, they were living it, which was as untrue for them as it is for us. Another reason was a failure to have an accountability group."[46]

I've recently been praying for several people who are facing daunting challenges—my prayer is that they would finish well. No one knows how much time we have left. I think I may still have 25 years or so, but then again I may have just 25 days. That's not my greatest concern. My earnest desire is that I will finish well by loving the Lord, serving my family and fulfilling my calling to encourage others to keep the faith. I'm not done yet, but by God's grace I am seeking accountability to keep heading in the right direction.

46. Bob Buford, *Finishing Well* (Brentwood, TN: Integrity Publishers, 2004), p. 124.

"Let us fix our eyes on Jesus, the author and perfecter of our faith, who for the joy set before him endured the cross, scorning its shame, and sat down at the right hand of the throne of God. Consider him who endured such opposition from sinful men, so that you will not grow weary and lose heart" (Hebrews 12:2-3).

Application Questions

1. Think about your life and ministry. What is delighting you? What is draining you? What are you pursuing? What are you avoiding? What are you discovering? How can this information help you pursue transformation more strategically and effectively?

2. Name one person who sharpens you. Name one person who deepens you. Name one person who resources you. Name one person who connects you. For who are you fulfilling those roles?

3. On a scale of 1 (deny it) to 10 (embrace it), to what degree do you submit yourself to the accountability of your elders? How would you describe your personal and professional relationships with them? If not healthy, what can you do to improve your relationship with the elders?

4. To whom are you willingly vulnerable regarding your thoughts, actions, and relationships? What mechanism do you use to confess your temptations, struggles, failures, and successes?

5. If you could write your own script, what would it look like for you to finish well – in your life, your family, and your ministry? What are the key components of finishing well in each area? What specific things do you need to do, stop doing, or do differently in order to finish well?

Group Discussion Questions

1. Which of the following best describes you? a) I actively avoid deep friendships, b) I am not interested in having a deep friendship, c) I am ambivalent regarding deep friendships, d) I am open to having a deep friendship, e) I want a deep friendship, f) I strongly desire a deep friendship.

2. Why do some people avoid and even undermine deep friendships? How does this tendency undermine their transformation efforts? What strategies can help people overcome these tendencies?

3. When is the last time you've been made aware of a significant blind spot? Who pointed it out to you? Did you receive the news about your blind spot well or did you argue, justify, or deny the blind spot? How did that information end up helping you?

4. What are the key ingredients of a relationship that encourages and rewards vulnerability? What can you do to infuse those ingredients in your most important relationships?

5. Who do you have in your life to ask hard questions about purity, addictions, relationships, and spiritual growth? What are the benefits of having someone to ask these questions? What are the dangers of not having someone to ask these questions?

TRANSFORMATION through MENTORING

LARRY TRAVIS

CHAPTER 10

MENTORING THAT TRANSFORMS

Leadership is hard work. It carries huge responsibility. Few are prepared for it. David Wheeler said," A leader must have the heart of a child, the mind of a scholar and the skin of a rhino." Leadership is not for the faint of heart. The fact is, leadership is where the buck stops. It most often makes the difference between success and failure. This is true in the home, in business, but most assuredly, in the church. Bill Hybels stated that the local church is the hope of the world and its future rests primarily in the hands of its leaders.

Here's something that leaders understand. Leaders come and go. Every leader has a time when they lead but soon enough, their time ends. And so, every leader must ask two questions:

1. What have I done to prepare the next generation to lead?

2. Who is going to take my place?

In Proverbs 27:17 Solomon writes, "As iron sharpens iron, so one man sharpens another" (KJV). This is called mentoring.

Hopefully you can recall men who have sharpened you—who have mentored you. I am thankful I have had many who taught me, challenged me, prayed for me, and loved me enough to help me to achieve what God had called me to do. The first man to mentor me was my father—Larry Travis, Sr. My Dad was a World War II veteran. He was from the "greatest generation."

He was a Master Sergeant in the Army and a trained B-52 bombardier. He was a great athlete who played with Ted Williams on the US Army baseball team and traveled throughout the US for a time entertaining troops. He was an Industrial Arts teacher and a state championship winning football coach. To say that life was structured around our house is a gross understatement.

But my Dad taught me many valuable lessons as a kid that would shape my life as a leader in the future. He taught me to treat people fairly, to be honest and true to your word, and that faith must make a difference in how you live. My Dad taught me a strong work ethic and if it was worth doing, it was worth doing right. My Dad loved to work more than he loved to breathe and he wanted his boys to catch his passion. We lived in Mt. Vernon, Kentucky—a very small town. The town mandated that every house in town connect to the new sewer system that was being implemented. The distance from the road to the back of our house was nearly 30 yards. The trench had to be four feet deep. A man came to our home and told our Dad that he had a backhoe and could dig the trench for $300. His response was—"Why do I need a backhoe when I have two diggers that live in my house—for FREE"—he emphasized to my brother and me. He smiled. We did not! My brother and I learned the value of hard work.

I also learned what it meant to mentor another man. My Dad was a football coach but in those days he had only one part time assistant coach to help. He did everything on the team which included coaching, gathering all the equipment each day, cleaning the locker room, making the schedules, getting uniforms cleaned, and even driving the boys home every afternoon after practice. Many times I would see him come home after a long day of teaching and practice well after 8pm—just to do it all over again the next day. I never understood what he was doing and the impact he was making until he passed away on February 6, 2015. Every player from his championship team and many, many others came to the funeral. Many flew in from all over the country to pay their respects and to share our sadness. To the man—they told us how he changed their lives—how he loved them and helped them become the men they are now. Dad not only mentored me but he showed me how to mentor others.

Another man that poured into me was a minister named Ronnie Sams. He's a Johnson University graduate. Now, I have to admit while growing up

I thought church was a bit boring, but then Ronnie came as the minister to our church in Mt. Vernon, Ky. He was young—in his late 20's at the time. He was athletic. I had never seen a young, athletic preacher before. And he was funny—especially in the pulpit. He loved to laugh and he loved hearing others laugh in church too. He made the Bible come alive. But the best part was that he wanted a friendship with me—this young, high school student who didn't have a clue about most things. And so, Ronnie began spending time with me. Almost every Sunday during my senior year of high school, he would invite me over to his house to play ping-pong in his basement. We would play nearly 40 games a Sunday. It was during those times we would talk—about everything. He never pushed. He just shared and I listened. Oh, how I listened. I went into the ministry because of what Ronnie Sams taught me about life, and faith, and pouring into others. I got to tell him a few years ago what he meant to me. He cried…so did I.

Here's what every leader should remember. Mentoring changes other people's lives but best of all—it changes yours! Indeed—mentoring transforms!

DEFINITION OF MENTORING

So what is mentoring? The Apostle Paul gives us a beautiful picture of mentoring found in 1 Thessalonians 2:7-12.

> We were like young children among you. Just as a nursing mother cares for her children, so we cared for you, because we loved you so much, we were delighted to share with you not only the gospel of God but our lives as well. Surely you remember, brothers and sisters, our toil and hardship, we worked night and day in order not to be a burden to anyone while we preached the gospel of God to you. You are witnesses, and so is God, of how holy, righteous and blameless we were among you who believed. For you know that we dealt with each of you as a father deals with his own children, encouraging, comforting and urging you to live lives worthy of God, who calls you into his kingdom and glory.

Spiritual parenting-mentoring brings together into one relationship the call, the grace, and the love to be transformed to the image and mission of Christ. So, mentoring is the pouring of the mentor's life into the protégé's life for the purpose of transformation and growth. Here are some ways that some protégés define mentoring:

Drew Thurman: "Mentoring means receiving spiritual guidance, faith-based knowledge, and critical life skills through a one-on-one relationship with a mentor. Mentoring has been the single greatest factor in my personal growth and transformation as a spiritual leader and a huge factor in my sanctification process. Through investment, modeling, and coaching, I've been given the direction to become things that I didn't know how to be on my own. The beauty of the mentoring relationship is that it allows me to live life in connection with someone with more life experience and knowledge and who models what life looks like in future stages."

Scott Solemine: "Mentoring is when a man in his own journey reaches backward toward another to bring perspective, experience and lessons learned along the way. I have seen firsthand the benefit of hearing from a man of God who is going through the journey of ministry. Each mentor has helped to bridge the conceptual truth of God's Word into the practical application of it. My mentor has helped me see over the tree line when I have asked questions like—Am I a young fool-what do I need to learn from this? These questions have helped me bring clarity to my world and ministry in a bigger way. People have often said, "You speak beyond your years." It is not my voice but the collective investments of men who have deposited into my life by the grace of God."

Tim Captain: "Mentoring is shepherding someone towards their God-given purpose through years of shared life and experience. Mentoring has helped me discover the necessity of ongoing spiritual sustenance. My relationship with my mentor has helped me to persevere in hope and keep my eyes heavenward-towards

Christ. The greatest value of being mentored is the relationship. The 'phone a friend' fall back option is incredibly important in ministry and life. Mentoring has encouraged risk-taking in obedience to God while speaking into my life with measured wisdom. It has freed me from the fear of being frozen by failure. Every good church has a discipleship plan but leaders are often expected to 'self-disciple.' But I need to be challenged, prayed over, laughed with, cried with and treated as a person in need of the love of Jesus. I absolutely need mentoring."

Rob Powell: "Mentoring is gaining wisdom from a relatable person who has experienced many things you have not but are likely to face. Mentoring improves my decisions and prepares me to make a difference in someone else's life."

Garrett Schrantz: "Mentoring is listening and learning from others who can offer guidance whether it be for a specific issue or just general advice to keep you on track. It is important for a mentor to share they were not always perfect and understand the protégé will not be either. A mentor is more influential when they share what they have done incorrectly."

Dustin Dalton: "Mentoring is the process of giving wisdom and insight through the context of relationship. It requires time, effort and specific goals. It is commitment. It's hard to find people to minister to you. Mentoring has done that for me. They have modeled for me true Christ-like behavior. It has prepared me for the future. The best part of mentoring is friendship. Mentoring is an intentional thing. As John Maxwell said, 'You do not become a mentor by accident'."

Jeremy Lawson: "Mentoring is about having a friend who is a few steps ahead of you in life. He is a sounding board, a coach, a cheerleader all at the same time. A mentor is someone who cares enough to listen, to challenge, to encourage, to pray and speak truths into your life. The greatest value of mentoring is to know that someone cares. I am a wiser, more patient and persistent leader because of the mentoring I have received."

Nate Sallee: "Mentoring is when a person sees the value of building into people as they see the vision of the long-term impact. If I don't have mentors in my life, I am short circuiting what God has for me. It robs myself of the wisdom for the next generation. The great value of being mentored is confidence—knowing you know you are not alone and you know your mentor has been faithful going down the path longer than you have. The best part of mentoring is that God believes it's a good idea."

So mentoring is–Sharing. Giving. Teaching. Praying. Building. Loving. Purpose-filled. Intentional. Mentoring is to be transforming both for the protégé and the mentor.

MENTORING VERSES DISCIPLESHIP

Mentoring is somewhat different than discipleship. Jesus called men to follow him. As they followed, they learned. The word disciple means "learner." Then Jesus challenged those same men to "go and make disciples of all nations." Discipleship is always about knowing Christ; becoming like Christ in every area of a person's life. It affects who we are and how we live each day.

While mentoring is a part of discipleship, it is different. Discipleship is about mastering the goal of becoming mature in Christ. It is about learning about God and the Kingdom. It is about sharing the "good news" with the world so they too can follow Christ. Mentoring is more about the needs of the protégé. It involves a long -term relationship that helps the protégé follow His calling from God and accomplish what God has purposed in his life.

So in other words, discipleship focuses on the leader's agenda, content, spiritual disciplines, and academics. Discipleship only requires respect. Mentoring focuses on the protégés agenda, whole life counsel, and practical life experience. Mentoring requires a personal relationship. Discipleship often can be accomplished in short term teachings while mentoring often requires a long-term commitment of mentor to the protégé.

THE NEED FOR MENTORING

When Jesus began his ministry, His first order of business was to select men who would later lead the beginnings of the church. He would disciple them but He would also mentor them. He would walk beside them and live life with them. He developed them into the leaders that would turn the world upside down. Max DePree, author of *Leadership is an Art*, stated, "Succession is one of the key responsibilities of leadership."[47] John Maxwell aptly states, "Achievement comes to someone when he is able to do great things for himself. Success comes when he empowers followers to do great things with him. Significance comes when he develops leaders to do great things for him. But a legacy is created only when a person puts his organization into the position to do great things without him."[48] This occurs when the baton of leadership is passed along to the next generation.

Question. How necessary is it that present leaders disciple, train, teach, and mentor the next generation so they are ready to take up the mantle? Let's begin by noting some statistics about the state of the church in America.

- Only 52 million people in America are in church on any given weekend.

- The 52 million represents about 17% of Americans.

- From 1990-2006 America averaged about 52 million in church and so attendance has been stagnant while American has grown another 53 million in population.

- Every state in America, except Hawaii, has decreased in attendance in church attendance from 1990 to 2010.

- There is an annual church closure rate in America of 4.2%.

Ed Stetzer's book, *Lost and Found*, offers these statistics:[49]

- 74% of millennials are going to no church of any kind.
- 82% believe in heaven.

47. See John Maxwell, *Leadership 101: What Every Leader Needs to Know* (Nashville, TN: Thomas Nelson, 2002), p. 104.
48. Ibid., 104-105.
49. Ed Stetzer, *Lost and Found* (Nashville, TN: B&H Publishing Group, 2009).

- 60% believe in hell.
- 66% believe Jesus died and resurrected.
- 77% believe Jesus could make a positive difference in their lives.

The Center for Church Leadership's research has revealed these statistics:

- 1500 ministers leave the ministry every month due to moral failure, financial stresses, and contention in the church.

- 80% of ministers feel unqualified as a leader.

- 90% of ministers feel unprepared.

- 70% of ministers feel underpaid.

- After 3 years of ministry, only 50% of ministers feel called of God to minister.

The most haunting quote of the survey conducted by the Center was this—"I feel like I am doing ministry all alone."

Here's some good news and positive statistics gathered from Thom Rainer's book, *The Millennials*. He writes that 40 percent of adult Millennials currently have a mentor in their lives.[50] This means that for every five Millennials, two are connected with a mentor. These statistics emphatically state that Millennials desire mentors and are open to the opportunities.

So there is a great need for more church leaders in America. The next generation of leaders is open to being trained, taught, encouraged, and loved by mentors. But this process is not about a program. It is about a heart for the lost. It is about a heart for the next generation of leaders who can impact the nation and yes, the world. It is about caring enough for others that each person who has experience in life and ministry become willing and eager to pass along their wisdom and support to a generation willing to receive it. It is about raising up more leaders. It is about growing the church. The need is great and every minister needs to be motivated to inspire the next generation to take their place. May all who come behind us find us faithful!

---

50. Thom Rainer, *The Millennials* (Nashville, TN: B&H Publishing Group, 2011), p. 41.

THE GOAL OF MENTORING

In Matthew 28:19, 20, Jesus clearly commanded all Christians to go and make disciples. At the core of discipleship—and yes, mentoring, is transformation. The goal is to become like Christ—to mature in Christ. The goal of the mentor is to foster this transformation by the work of the Holy Spirit in each person's life. John Maxwell stated, "We teach what we know. We reproduce what we are."[51] As the Apostle Paul stated, "Follow my example, as I follow the example of Christ" (1 Corinthians 11:1). Make no mistake; this is the goal of every mentor. While we understand there will never be perfection, the goal is continual transformation. The mentor in the life of the protégé will create goals, or stair-steps if you please, toward Christ. He will give understanding, explanation, and will create accountability in this journey of maturity. The following quotes demonstrate the impact that mentors have had in the lives of protégés.

Scott Solimine: "My mentor has shown to me the sacrifice and determination that true manhood entails. I have gained resources and tools that I can use every day."

Garrett Schrantz: "The greatest value is the feeling of knowing you are loved and supported. It has given me the courage and motivation to push forward when I felt like quitting or giving less effort."

Drew Thurman: "I have amazing parents but I needed people beyond me to teach me what a husband looks like, what a father looks like, what a minister looks like and how to handle what life throws at me."

Tim Captain: "Mentoring at its best is the giving and receiving of God's grace in my life."

Rob Powell: "Because I understand my mentor is not so different from me, I understand with discipline I am capable of similar accomplishments."

51. John Maxwell, *Maxwell Daily Reader* (Nashville, TN: Thomas Nelson, 2007), p. 336.

Dustin Dalton: "Being mentored has given me validation as I have walked through rough patches in ministry. God has worked through the shepherding voices to affirm my pastoral calling. I don't know where I would be if my mentor would not have asked me—So, have you ever thought about preaching? God used that question to plant a seed that led me to my calling in ministry."

GARRETT'S STORY

I met Garrett Schrantz on his first day of college at Northern Kentucky University. He was taking my Introduction to Communication class. He sat in the second seat from the front, middle row. Garrett was a pitcher on the NKU baseball team. I discovered that from the initial introductions from everyone in the class. In this particular communication class there were many varied discussions because of the speeches that were given in class. Often after class and sometimes before, we would talk about our interests, school load, and the team. I shared with him about my father who played professional baseball and we would talk about how he was doing with all the demands of being an elite student-athlete in a D-1 baseball program.

Later in the fall, 2013, I invited everyone in my classes to the Drug House Odyssey program at Nicholson Christian Church where I was ministering. After class he immediately said he was interested in going. Another student came along too. Before I hosted him at the event, we went out to eat. Little did I know that would be the first meal of many to follow over the next four years.

At the beginning of the next semester we began meeting every other week for supper. One topic of discussion led to another and then, of course, to our spiritual lives. Garrett had grown up Catholic. He had gone to Catholic schools and so he had a faith in God. However, his foundation was weak and his understanding of how God wanted to work in his life was misunderstood and disconnected. It was more about how he felt than what he believed. He didn't know how and why God wanted to affect his life every day.

I would attend every NKU baseball game with a special interest when he pitched. I was more nervous than he was. Our friendship began to grow and so did our conversations. We both opened up our lives to each other. His parents had divorced and that had dramatically impacted him and his brothers and sister. He was loved and guided by both parents but there was lots of freedom that led to many lifestyle choices that he has questioned since that time. In our conversations, we would often talk about life, his girlfriend, his future goals, baseball, fears, joys, and of course, faith. He had never dreamed of having a friendship with a minister. I hadn't thought so much of having a close friendship again with a college student. We are separated by 40 years in age, but it became a friendship that has meant more to both of us than can be explained.

The ultimate goal to me in our friendship was for Garrett to know that Jesus was in his life and that Jesus wanted to guide him and transform him into what God wanted. I would often tell him, "God has great plans for you." I would ask questions and listen to him. He would ask questions and listen to me. He came to church at times. I asked Garrett, "Do you know, if you would die, would you go to heaven?" He responded, "Maybe—I hope so." I told him that you can know for sure and we talked about him accepting Christ as his personal Savior. On November 13, 2014, I immersed Garrett at Nicholson Christian Church. He has lived for Christ every day since—like the rest of us, not perfection—but with a right heart toward God.

I asked Garrett to go on a mission trip with me to the Philippines in May, 2015. It was there he shared his faith story with a number of groups and churches. Everywhere we went both teens and adults flocked to him to hear more about his life and faith. In March, 2016, we traveled to Russia and the Crimea. In May, 2017, we traveled to Kenya and Rome. With each trip I could see his heart change, his faith grow, and his relationship with Jesus deepen. These trips had purpose as I would challenge him to open up, share his faith, serve more and see what God had in store for him. Garrett grew from a self-focus to a focus on others and the world. His thinking about today changed. He began learning from his past and the effect it has on his present. He began living in the present and the purpose of each day and how that connected to his life now. Garrett began making plans for the future that included professional, physical, relational and spiritual goals. He changed from being self-reliant to a dependence upon God. His prayers have grown to reflect a real relationship with the Lord.

In March of 2016 I received a letter from Garrett. He would always write me a letter on my birthday. In that letter he thanked me for the support I had given him but he thanked me for being his mentor, his teacher, his friend. He explained that he knew he would not be the man he was without our time together. Through the years it was an experience that changed my life—and his—as we watched God work to accomplish His purpose in our lives. It was a step-by-step process that involved meals, conversations, rounds of golf, meals, prayer times, trips, movies, and did I mention meals?!

In response to the mentoring, Garrett replied, "The gift of mentoring is one I know I can never repay to Larry and yet I know God put us in each other's lives for a reason. Because of his example I know I want to give this truly invaluable gift to others and I can only hope it will enrich their lives as much as it has mine." Garrett has retained the essence of himself that God put in him from the beginning but he has allowed God to continue to mold him as he has been guided, encouraged and loved. He'll never be the same and I will never be the same either! For Garrett—the best is yet to come! This mentor-protégé relationship has been a great example of what God can do when people are committed to a friendship that is meant to grow both people so they can accomplish everything God directs.

What I have learned from this relationship and a few others as a mentor, is that mentoring has become the most fulfilling part of my ministry. It is the investment of my life into another life that changes both. True transformation takes place because there is an innate challenge to both people to follow Christ in a real way and to keep each other accountable to that goal. The mentoring process helps both the mentor and protégé to stay on track because of the relationship tie. It is both planned and natural at the same time. It is intentional but life simply takes over in a caring way. It's never forced but open to what God has in store.

So Garrett's story is both his story and mine at the same time. Mentoring transforms us and it is there the call is revealed, the grace is given to be real, the love is shared to keep each other on track and ultimately your lives are never the same. This is the experience of mentoring that will leave you in awe of what God can do when we are in true fellowship with each other—when we care enough to pour ourselves into someone else for the good of both so they each can honor God! Mentoring doesn't take any special skills. It simply requires a person to care for another to reach the heights of what God has placed in them!

Here's what everyone needs to know—Mentoring Transforms!

Application Questions

1. Who has been your most influential mentor? What were the three most important lessons you learned from that person? How are those things contributing to your ministry today?

2. What strategies are you using to replicate yourself? How much time and energy are you dedicating each week to invest in next-generation leaders?

3. Who are you mentoring in a structured way? Who are you grooming to take your place?

4. In what ways are leadership, discipleship, and mentoring related? In what ways are they different? How well, and in what ways, are you accomplishing each in your ministry context?

5. In what ways are you experiencing joy, fulfillment, and growth as a result of mentoring other people?

Group Discussion Questions

1. Name one positive trait that you possess as a result of someone else's influence. How did that person mentor you? Was it formalized or casual? How would you and your life be different if that person had not invested in you?

2. In which of the following areas is mentoring most helpful? a) Leadership development, b) Skill acquisition, c) Knowledge acquisition, d) Financial management, e) Spiritual growth. For which of those areas do you have a formalized mentoring relationship?

3. What are some common reasons why most people don't have a mentor? What are some strategies and messages that could overcome those hurdles?

4. Who is currently serving as your mentor? Is that person helping you achieve transformation? If no, or if you don't have one, who do you already know and respect enough to ask to serve as your mentor?

5. Name three people who are already in your sphere of influence that you could mentor. What would be a natural way to begin investing in those people?

CHAPTER 11

THE BIBLICAL BASIS FOR MENTORING

N ate Sallee says, "The best part of mentoring for me is that God thinks it's a good idea." Each mentor needs to know that mentoring is biblically based and scripturally sound.

SCRIPTURES

Proverbs 27:17: "As iron sharpens iron, so one person sharpens another."

2 Timothy 2:2: "And the things you have heard me say in the presence of many witnesses entrust to reliable people who will also be qualified to teach others."

1 Thessalonians 2:7-8: "Just as a nursing mother cares for her children, so we cared for you, because we loved you so much, we were delighted to share with you not only the gospel of God but our lives as well."

1 Thessalonians 2:11-12: "For you know that we dealt with each of you as a father deals with his own children, encouraging, comforting, and urging you to live lives worthy of God, who calls you into his kingdom and glory."

Luke 6:40: "But everyone who is fully trained will be like his teacher."

1 Corinthians 4:16: "I urge you to imitate me."

1 Corinthians 11:1: "Follow my example as I follow the example of Christ."

2 Timothy 3:10: "You, however, know all about my teaching, my way of life, my purpose, faith, patience, love and endurance. "

Hebrews 13:7: "Remember your leaders, who spoke the word of God to you. Consider the outcome of their way of life and imitate their faith."

Philippians 3:17: "Join with others in following my example, brothers, and take note of those who live according to the pattern we gave you."

2 Thessalonians 3:9: "We did this, not because we do not have the right to such help, but in order to make ourselves a model for you to follow."

MENTORING IN THE BIBLE

Often when we think of teaching and training in the Bible, we often think of discipleship. Jesus did say, "Go and make disciples." But the question begs to be asked—how did He expect his followers to do that? Seminars often teach patterns that can be duplicated by teachers and their students. Knowledge is gained and the more we learn of God, the more we can become like Him. However, nothing changes the heart of a person more quickly and dramatically than to see the life-pattern in front of you. The idea is to not simply be taught but to be shown what it looks like in life. This is accomplished most effectively in mentoring as the mentor spends time with the protégé. There are many examples of this both in the Old Testament and in the New Testament.

Old Testament Mentoring Examples

1. *Jethro and Moses*: Exodus 18. Moses learns about delegation.

2. *Moses and Joshua*: Deuteronomy 31:1-8. Joshua watches Moses and prepares to lead Israel into the Promised Land.

3. *Moses and Caleb*: Numbers 13, 14:6-9, 34:16-19. Joshua 14:6-5. Moses mentors Caleb into leadership. He teaches about believing God's promises.

4. *Samuel and Saul*: 1 Samuel 9-15. Samuel teaches Saul, confronts Saul to repent and come back to God.

5. *Samuel and David*: 1 Samuel 16, 19:18-24. David is anointed by Samuel. Then, Samuel hides David from Saul.

6. *Jonathan and David*: 1 Samuel 18:1-4, 19:1-7, 20:1-42. David and Jonathan mentor one another. This is an example of peer mentoring.

7. *Elijah and Elisha*: 1 Kings 19:16-21, 2 Kings 2:1-16, 3:11. Elijah recruits Elisha to be his successor and teaches him about leadership.

New Testament Mentoring Examples

1. *Barnabas and Saul/Paul*: Acts 4:36-37, 9:26-30, 11:22-30. Barnabas leads Saul after his conversion into a connection with the church.

2. *Barnabas and John Mark:* Acts 15:36-39, 2 Timothy 4:11. After leaving Paul, Barnabas worked with John Mark. Later John Mark authored the book of Mark.

3. *Paul and Timothy*: Acts 16:1-3, Philippians 2:19-23, 1 and 2 Timothy. Timothy traveled with Paul on a missionary journey. Timothy ministered to Paul and later was the minister at Ephesus.

4. *Paul and Titus*: 2 Corinthians 7:6, 13-15, 8:17. Titus. Paul and Barnabas won Titus to Christ. They traveled together and later Titus became a minister in Crete.

5. Jesus and the Apostles

Mentoring was a valuable tool in both the Old Testament and in the New Testament, used to share leadership skills, shape character, and encourage their protégé for the challenges ahead. In each example, the relationship formed was a strong bond that helped both the mentor and protégé move forward with what God had called them to accomplish. The friendship and love was undeniable as a gift each to the other that fulfilled their lives and ministry. So, it is not only important to know that mentoring took place in the Bible but to know what it looked like so each present-day mentor and protégé can make it happen in their lives.

The story of Elijah and Elisha is found in 1 and 2 Kings. Elijah had enjoyed a great triumph over the prophets of Baal on Mount Carmel but shortly afterwards, he found himself in the depths of depression. He says," I am the only one and now they are trying to kill me too" (1 Kings 19:14).

This is what the Lord says in response:

> Go back the way you came, and go to the Desert of Damascus. When you get there, anoint Hazael king over Aram. Also, anoint Jehy son of Nimshi king over Israel, and anoint Elisha son of Shphat frm Abel Meholah to succeed you as prophet. Jehu will put to death any who escape the sword of Hazael, and Elisha will put to death any who escape the sword of Jehu. Yet I reserve seven thousand in Israel—all whose knees have not bowed down to Baal and whose mouths have not kissed him (1 Kings 19:15-18).

Now that is quite a backup plan! Here's what follows:

> So Elijah went from there and found Elisha son of Shaphat. He was plowing with twelve yoke of oxen, and he himself was driving the twelfth pair. Elijah went up to him and threw his cloak around him. Elisha then left his oxen and ran after Elijah. "Let me kiss my father and mother goodbye," he said, "and then I will come with you." "Go back," Elijah replied, "What have I done to you?" So Elisha left him and went back. He took his yoke of oxen and slaughtered them. He burned the plowing equipment to cook the meat and gave it to the people, and they

ate. Then he set out to follow Elijah and became his servant"
(1 Kings 19:19-21).

Elijah prays…"Lord, who will take my place?" And God gives him
Elisha. At this point note several points in the mentoring process. First, Elijah
challenged Elisha to follow. God had placed this desire in him and he followed
but it was going to cost him. Later, Jesus would say—So, you want to be my
disciple? Then pick up your cross. Elisha destroyed his way of life—killed his
livestock—burned the plows—gave it all away and then followed Elijah.

God will use the person who follows without conditions. Often the price
of following is heavy but the reward is great. Elisha learned this important
lesson—you learn how to be a great leader by first being a great follower.

2 Kings 2:1-3 says, "When the Lord was about to take Elijah up to heaven
in a whirlwind, Elijah and Elisha were on their way to Gilgal. Elijah said to
Elisha—'Stay here, the Lord has sent me to Bethel.' But Elisha said—'As
surely as the Lord lives and as you live, I will not leave you.' So they went
down to Bethel. The company of the prophets at Bethel came out to Elisha
and asked, 'Do you know that the Lord is going to take your master from you
today?' 'Yes, I know,' Elisha replied—'so be quiet.'"

Elisha was hurting. His mentor was going to be taken and he would be
on his own. But Elisha had one more gift to ask from his mentor. It was an
amazing ask!

> When they had crossed, Elijah said to Elisha, "Tell me, what
> can I do for you before I am taken from you?" "Let me inherit a
> double portion of your spirit," Elisha replied. "You have asked a
> difficult thing," Elijah said, "yet if you see me when I am taken
> from you, it will be yours—otherwise, it will not." As they were
> walking along and talking together, suddenly a chariot of fire
> and horses of fire appeared and separated the two of them, and
> Elijah went up to heaven in a whirlwind. Elisha saw this and
> cried out, "My father! My father! The chariots and horsemen
> of Israel." And Elisha saw him no more…The company of the
> prophets from Jericho who were watching, said, "The spirit of
> Elijah is resting on Elisha." (2 Kings 2:9-12a; 15a).

This is mentoring at its finest. This is passing the baton of leadership and ministry from the mentor to the protégé. John Maxwell says, "A leader's lasting value is measured by succession."[52] Leaders often talk about the legacies they wish to leave behind them. One of the definitions of legacy is the word—inheritance. The greatest inheritance any leader could leave for the church are the leaders that have been trained and mentored.

Here's the story of a modern day Elijah. His name is Sasha. He lives in the Ukraine. He works six days a week and he preaches each Sunday at two churches that are three hours apart by train. A few years ago I stayed at his house on a short-term mission trip. One night after dinner I asked Sasha to tell me his story—to tell me what it was like being a Christian during the Communist regime in the former Soviet Union. He stood—turned away—but when he turned back, he did so with tears in his eyes. He said to me, "So you really want to know?" I said, "yes." He then told me about the ten years he had spent in prison for being a Christian—one time for two years because he had not covered his Bible in public. He told me about other Christians in his apartment complex that had been kidnapped and the parents had never seen their children again. The tears began streaming down his face as he thought about the hardships that had been endured by him, his family and by others but with a gritty determination he then said to me, "They could take our freedom. They could take our children. But they could not take our faith."

When we finished the discussion a few moments later, Sasha then took me to a meeting where he introduced me to a number of young men that he had mentored during the Communist regime. Each of them was leading churches and sharing the gospel. The joy of his heart could be not contained by the smile on his face and the satisfaction in his spirit. He knew the ministry would go forward and the Lord was pleased. All the hardships had been worth it all!

---

52. John Maxwell, *The 21 Most Powerful Minutes in a Leader's Day* (Nashville, TN: Thomas Nelson, 2000). p. 351.

Application Questions

1. Consider Hebrews 13:7. Identify a living mentor who was particularly influential in your life. Hand-write a note to that person that describes the impact they had on you and the specific ways that you are modeling their lifestyle and ministry.

2. Consider Proverbs 27:17. How does sharpening relate to mentoring? In what ways is the sharpening process painful and difficult? In what ways is the sharpening process essential for transformation to take place?

3. Consider Luke 6:40. If the goal is to be "fully trained," what specific areas do you still need to work on in order to achieve that standard? Who do you know and respect that can mentor you in those areas? When will you contact that person?

4. Consider 1 Thessalonians 2:11-12. When you mentor other people, are you most naturally inclined to listen, encourage, comfort, or hold them accountable? Is it essential for a mentor to accomplish all four things? Why or why not? Is there a natural priority among those four tasks?

5. Consider 1 Corinthians 11:1. How well are you reflecting Christ to those who look up to you? How are you modeling Jesus' character and mission in your interactions with those who you are mentoring? Are there any areas that you need to improve in to effectively mentor others?

Group Discussion Questions

1. Consider Luke 6:40. Who was your favorite school teacher? What grade did that person teach? Why was that teacher your favorite? In what ways did you want to be like that teacher?

2. Consider 1 Thessalonians 2:7-8. To what degree is it important for a mentor to have a personal relationship with the protégé? How does demonstrating love, care, and compassion enhance the mentoring process? What are the consequences if a mentor does not obviously care for the protégé?

3. Consider 2 Timothy 3:10. For which of the following areas do you most need mentoring? a) Life, b) purpose, c) faith, d) patience, e) love, f) endurance. In what ways do you think mentoring would increase your happiness, fulfillment, and success?

4. Consider 2 Thessalonians 3:9. To what degree do you think of yourself as a mentor? In what areas are you most naturally qualified to mentor someone? What do you most commonly model through your words and actions, whether productive or unproductive?

5. Consider 2 Timothy 2:2. To whom are you entrusting your wisdom, experience, skill, and knowledge? In what ways are you training and encouraging them to teach other people? Why is this replication important for the Church and the world?

CHAPTER 12

15 CHARACTERISTICS OF MENTORING

Mentoring is not a program. It's a relationship. Mentoring is not a lot of do's and don'ts. It's a friendship that feeds both the mentor and protégé. Mentoring is about pouring oneself into another with the goal of helping a person reach their potential in life and calling. So, what does mentoring look like? What do the characteristics of a caring friendship look like as one person mentors another? While no relationship possesses all of these in abundance, each one is necessary for the relationship to grow and deepen so true change—by God's grace and power—can occur in both lives.

CHARACTERISTIC 1: OPENNESS

"If we confess our sins, he is faithful and just and will forgive us our sins and purify us from all unrighteousness" (1 John 1:9).

Openness is the willingness to be vulnerable. It is sharing the good, the bad, and the ugly of your life with another person knowing they will not judge you. It is the sharing of your heart and soul with another. Openness requires courage and trust. This happens in the deepening of the relationship.

> *Drew Thurman*: When I was first mentored I was uncomfortable with the level of openness and honesty. My mentor was transparent and vulnerable and he expected me to be the same. There is a direct correlation between and level of transparency and effectiveness in mentoring. After time, I became more comfortable.

Scott Solemine: Months before I took the Lead Pastor role at my church, I wanted to share some ideas with my mentor but after a few weeks I wanted to shift those plans. I remember being nervous making that call and discuss a new focus. I didn't want to frustrate him because of the time he had invested. But the call was quite different than I expected. He helped me think dynamically about the plans for the future. There were no feelings about wasted time. This openness to the type of leader I am was truly empowering.

Tim Captain: I cannot count how many meals I have had with my mentor. While there were scheduled meetings, a lot of time was spent just dropping in, eating a meal, playing golf or attending an event. All of this led to natural openness.

Nate Sallee: My mentor would be open and honest about his struggles. He shared how he overcame his struggles and that helped me lead better.

Garrett Schrantz: My mentor is someone I knew I could tell anything and not be judged. The openness has made the process of mentoring easier and more valuable.

CHARACTERISTIC 2: INTEGRITY

"In my integrity you uphold me and set me in your presence" (Psalm 41:12).
"The integrity of the upright guides them" (Proverbs 11:3).
Integrity is not only telling the truth about what is happening in your life, it is being true to your word. It is keeping your promises to yourself and to your mentor/protégé. It is following through with the commitments that have been made each to the other.

Drew Thurman: I have tried to model my mentor in my mentoring to others. A recent year-long intern commented in his evaluation that the biggest thing he had learned from me was what I had allowed him to see in my own life. I allowed him to see my passion for ministry, the pain of a miscarriage and my deep focus on being a Godly husband. He said these reoriented his life, leadership and marriage.

Scott Solemine: Honesty from my mentor has helped me see if I am acting out of immaturity or foolishness. I have asked-Am I missing something? I knew I would get a straight answer. One time I had a difficult situation to handle in my church. I was doubting myself and my heart. But my mentor said, "You can't do that." Then he said, " It's never wrong to do the right thing." I don't always need encouragement or affirmation. I need my mentor to be straight with me.

Tim Captain: My mentor and I were very honest with each other even to the point we could be rather cutting at times. We decided to spur one another on to love and good deeds. Speaking the truth in love is hard to come by.

Garrett Schrantz: It has been important to share with my mentor differences of opinion about faith, church, and politics. We each have grown from what the other person had to share.

Rob Powell: It is not until the protégé sees the mentor as a genuine person they can share a mutual trust. Everyone is flawed and you don't come to really appreciate and understand any person without seeing their flaws and accepting them.

Dustin Dalton: I was attending Cedarville. I sat down with my mentor and he talked honestly with me about my school debt and the effect of that debt. He felt like he could speak into my life and future. I transferred schools and it was one of the best decisions of my life.

CHARACTERISTIC 3: TIME

"Be very careful, then, how you live—not as unwise but as wise, making the most of every opportunity, because the days are evil" (Ephesians 5:15-16). Time might be today's most precious commodity and in the mentoring relationship, it is the most valuable. Quality time is important but there needs to be an adequate amount of time given in the relationship to make it work.

> *Drew Thurman*: Quote from Tony Dungy, "If you want to make a difference in the lives of people you lead, you must be willing to walk alongside them, spend time with them, not shout down at them from on high."

> *Scott Solemine*: The time that was devoted to me was intentional time. Questions were answered. Examples given. I am amazed at the time he invested in me.

> *Tim Captain:* While I learned from many, my mentor was there. He got to know my friends, listened, laughed, traveled together and led together. He saw me on good days and bad days. I asked questions about ministry and fatherhood. Those questions come up when you have spent time together. If I didn't trust his character, love of God and family, then I wouldn't have asked about his thoughts on fatherhood when I needed it. Trust is built with time.

> *Jeremy Lawson*: The mentor relationship is not about the quantity of time but the quality. One interrupted lunch every few months means more than a weekly visit where both are distracted.

> *Nate Sallee*: Time is the most valuable resource in the mentor relationship. Trust takes time. Car rides and organic conversations are a great place to process things.

CHARACTERISTIC 4: INVESTMENT OF LIFE

"Because of the service by which you have proved yourselves, others will praise God for the obedience that accompanies your confession of the gospel of Christ, and for your generosity in sharing with them and with everyone else" (2 Corinthians 9:13).

Mentoring requires the mentor to give time, resources, energy but it requires most of all—YOURSELF. As the Clemson Tigers say, "You have to be ALL IN!" John Sowers says, "Mentors win by showing up."

Drew Thurman: Mentoring relationships never follow a script. It is an intense investment. My mentor carved out time when it was inconvenient. He called—texted—emailed. He has been there for every important event in my life and the cumulative effect of investment and sacrifice is hard to fathom. How could my mentor's fingerprints not be all over my life.

Tim Captain: My mentor taught from the progressive shift from "I do, you watch" to "you do and teach." I traveled with my mentor as he consulted churches. First I drove and ran power points but later taught whole sections of the seminars. He could have chosen to do things on his own but the progression was natural and intentional.

Rob Powell: When a mentor invests his life in you he cements the understanding that you are not just a project. It shows the mentor enjoys spending time with you and a deeper relationship can develop.

Garrett Schrantz: Because of the investment of life into me by my mentor, I truly wish to pass on the gift of mentoring to others.

Jeremy Lawson: I have spent most of my life as a pastor investing in other people. There are times I felt drained. Having someone invest in me filled my cup back up so I could invest in others.

CHARACTERISTIC 5: SACRIFICE

"I urge you brothers and sisters, in view of God's mercy, to offer your bodies as a living sacrifice, holy and pleasing to God—this is your true and proper worship. Do not conform to the pattern of this world, but be transformed by the renewing of your mind" (Romans 12:1-2).

Sacrifice is giving up something you love, for someone you love more. It is giving up something valuable and important that will bring more joy to the protégé when you give it to them than it did to the mentor. This could be time, energy, resources but ultimately it means you are giving up –at least at times—your desires for theirs.

Tim Captain: I am not sure of the sacrifices my mentor has made for me over the years. I mostly feel blessed because of his generosity with his life.

Jeremy Lawson: There are a million things my mentor could have been doing at any given moment. When there is a cost involved in mentoring, it carries a lot of weight in your life.

Andrew Bernardez: I didn't realize how much sacrifice would be a part of a mentoring relationship until I was a mentor. I realize the mentor sacrifices but the protégé must sacrifice as well—time, resources, energy.

CHARACTERISTIC 6: TRUTH

"It gave me great joy to have some brothers come and tell about your faithfulness to the truth and how you continue to walk in the truth" (3 John 3).

Jesus is the truth. He stands for what is real and lasting—for that which matters now and for eternity. Truth is the reality of Jesus that binds the relationship beyond the bonds of friendship and mutual goals.

Tim Captain: There are moments of truth that stick with you for a long time. I was worried about raising money for a mission trip. My mentor said to me, "God will never call you to do something that God does not provide for." I have learned to connect my living with the trust I have in God.

Nate Sallee: Too many times we can be overly optimistic and even in denial that something is going just fine. When a mentor has the guts to speak 100% into you it can unlock new levels of growth.

CHARACTERISTIC 7: EXPERIENCES

"Paul came to Derbe and then to Lystra, where a disciple named Timothy lived." Acts 16:1, "When Paul and his companions had passed through Amphipolis and Apollonia, they came to Thessalonica, where there was a Jewish synagogue" (Acts 17:1).

As the mentor walks with his protégé, they will experience life together—the good and bad times. The protégé will learn how to handle life experiences as he watches the mentor live. Serving together—traveling together is a great teacher for both. It often is in this laboratory of life where the relationship deepens and memories are made that bind the two together.

Drew Thurman: Experiences bind people together. There is forever a bond that is forged. While I have golfed with my mentor, watched a sunset over the Grand Canyon, stood at the edge of Victoria Falls and served in the Dominican Republic, the living life alongside me is most valuable.

Tim Captain: I would not be serving a multicultural-multilingual church if it were not for my parents and my mentor. My family forged that in me but my mentor reinforced that. Because of my travels to four continents and the ministry that took place, I have been prepared to do the ministry I am doing right now. The trips that were jammed-packed took all the theoretical and made it powerfully real.

Rob Powell: Shared experiences make a good relationship—great. The experience together with my mentor helps me to know there is someone who can look back and feel the joy and sadness that was shared in that moment.

Dustin Dalton: One experience I had with my mentor was a trip to ICOM. I got to know my mentor and others. It made me feel a part of the church team and make my transition to full time ministry easier.

Jeremy Lawson: My rounds of golf with my mentor have been and are still invaluable to me.

Nate Sallee: I rose from my bunk in the DR and then I heard my mentor says, "Preaching in the DR! You ready for this Nate? It's going to be a ton of fun!" His enthusiasm set the tone for the day. My mentor knew I was ready because he had taught me, equipped me for that role and was happy to empower me to get after it. That is mentoring to me.

Andrew Bernardez: Nothing says more to me than a mentor sharing life experience with his protégé. My mentor traveled with me on mission trips and it helped me understand who I was as a leader. Our experiences have given me the chances to use what I have learned in an environment that was safe.

CHARACTERISTIC 8: PRAYER

"And in their prayers for you their hearts will go out to you, because of the surpassing grace God has given you" (2 Corinthians 9:14).

The realness of any mentoring relationship is forged in prayer—for each other and with each other. Your lives are exposed, your sins discovered/ forgiven, and Godly power is poured into each soul.

Drew Thurman: After I talk with my mentor he tells me every time, "I am praying for you every day." It's an amazing feeling knowing that someone is covering me with prayer every day. I know the successes I have will be due to the prayers my mentor offered on my behalf. Here's one prayer my mentor taught me. "God, I will preach your Word whenever, wherever, to whoever. Give me the opportunity and I will go." Ten years later I still pray that prayer and it has changed my life and calling.

Tim Captain: It is humbling to know someone is praying for you because it reminds you of the truth of God in you. More recently my mentor and I have asked each other, "How can I be praying for you?" This question is both an invitation and an action.

Rob Powell: It's great hearing someone say, "I am praying for you every day."

Garrett Schrantz: By listening to my mentor talk to God I have learned to talk to God in a way that allows me to build a personal relationship with him.

Jeremy Lawson: Prayer in the mentor relationship should be a two-way street. The person being mentored can return some of the investment by praying for his mentor too.

Nate Sallee: When my mentor told me he has a daily prayer list, it was super inspiring. It was cool to know that I was on that list.

CHARACTERISTIC 9: FRIENDSHIP

"A friend loves at all times, and a brother is born for adversity" (Proverbs 17:17).

At the core of every mentoring relationship is a deep, abiding friendship. You are there for each other emotionally and spiritually. You have fun together, you work together and accomplish goals together. Miles may separate a friendship but the unity of spirit will continue to guide and encourage.

Tim Captain: I have seen mentors who talked all the time. One of the things with my mentor is that he asks great questions and then listens. Asking open-ended, non-leading questions was a great way of exploring what was in my heart—and that's what great friends do.

Jeremy Lawson: Friendship is the element of the mentor relationship that has meant more to me than anything else. Having a friend that is cheering me on and has my back in all situations is truly life giving.

Nate Sallee: A great mentor needs to strike the balance of being a friend while maintaining the status of the one who has logged more miles in the trenches. An effective mentor creates a relationship that will last.

Andrew Bernardez: Friendship has probably been one of my favorite fruits of my mentoring relationships. My mentor knows me better than most so it's easy to come to him for encouragement. Hanging out with my mentors is easy and I enjoy spending time with them.

CHARACTERISTIC 10: ENCOURAGEMENT

"But now I urge you to keep up your courage" (Acts 27:22).

Encouragement is the building up of another. It is picking up the other when they have fallen down. It is the fuel of believing in the protégé that helps them believe in themselves that keeps them growing.

Drew Thurman: My mentor was one of the first to affirm and encourage me in my calling to preaching. He began to vision cast how that calling could be used in a manner well beyond what I could imagine. While God created a deep calling in my life, I needed a mentor to affirm it and push me towards my purpose.

Garrett Schrantz: When I was a sophomore in college, I decided to end my baseball career that had been everything to me. I had doubts and a lack of purpose during that time. My mentor often reminded me of God's purpose and spoke of leaning into my faith when I was uncertain about going down a new path.

Tim Captain: Speaking encouragement into another person is having a God-oriented conversation with someone that you are deeply connected to. There is encouragement when you are challenged to do something, to climb the next hill and know there is someone in your corner.

Rob Powell: I have been encouraged when my mentor suggests that I take on a task that I do not have the skills for. After accomplishing it, I have more confidence and realize I had more skills all along.

Nate Sallee: A mentor can speak life into those leading. My mentor after I wrote an FCA newsletter sent out a reply, "Proud of you Nate!" Those four words will stay with me!

CHARACTERISTIC 11: INSPIRATION

"But it is the spirit in the man, the breath of the Almighty, that gives him understanding" (Job 32:8).

To inspire another is to help them believe in themselves even when they don't believe it. It is helping the protégé see the potential that is in them—the vision that God had for their lives from the start.

> *Tim Captain:* I was often inspired with simple invitations to things that inspired my mentor. I was invited to sit in on leadership round tables that my mentor enjoyed and gave him insight. He would tell me about leaders that were inspiring him. While there were things that did not inspire me, the lesson was applied more broadly—how do I put myself in a position to be inspired by God and the leaders He is working through?

> *Rob Powell:* I have been inspired to be pushed to speak in the DR, to become a deacon and lead my aunt's funeral. It was all about people believing in me.

> *Dustin Dalton:* After I preached once, my mentor pointed out some specific gifts I have as a communicator. It helped me grow as a preacher and develop a method that is best with my giftedness.

> *Jeremy Lawson:* My best mentors are men that I look up to. They are examples of good fathers, husbands, ministers, leaders and men of God. For me the best inspiration is seeing an example lived out, seeing someone that I look at and say, "I want to be like that."

CHARACTERISTIC 12: CORRECTION

"Only be careful, and watch yourselves closely so you do not forget the things your eyes have seen or let them slip from your heart as long as you live. Teach them to your children and to their children after them" (Deuteronomy 4:9).

Every parent knows their child will make mistakes. It is the loving parent that carefully moves the child back on track so continued progress will be made. Every mentor must be given the right to correct the protégé. This right is earned through time, experience and trust.

Tim Captain: I need more in this area. I have a tendency to be hard headed and some not-so-subtle correction to steer me back on course.

Rob Powell: The relationship has to be on a high level for the mentor to pull this off.

Jeremy Lawson: Correction is difficult but essential. The mentor must have courage to present it and the protégé needs humility to accept it. The mentor needs to present it with humility and love, not ego. A person being mentored can tell the difference.

Nate Sallee: Correction is tied to love for me. While I don't want to be corrected all the time my mentor loved me enough to not passively allow things to continue that would threaten the health in my life or the church.

CHARACTERISTIC 13: SUPPORT

"Two are better than one, because they have a good return for their work. If one falls down, his friend can help him up. But pity the man who falls and has no one to help him up" (Ecclesiastes 4:9-10).

Most children know the support of a parent. Sometimes support is expected by the child. However, the support of the mentor often comes as a surprise to the protégé because no one is making them have this relationship. Support is not giving to the protégé whatever they want. It is giving them what they need at the right time. It is lifting them up so the journey continues.

Tim Captain: No one learned to walk a tightrope without a safety net. This is what the mentor does for his protégé. A mentor does not always keep the protégé from falling but my mentor has helped me take steps even after experiencing failure. This safety net has helped me risk without being frozen by fear.

Rob Powell: This characteristic of support has had a huge impact on me. Support is closely related to time. It seems insignificant because no action is really being accomplished but the value of knowing that someone is there for you when you need them cannot be overstated. Attending funerals, births, hospitals mean everything when a person is down. My mentor takes every opportunity to build me up in front of others and to tell others the great job I am doing at my work.

Dustin Dalton: My mentor has been there for me during a hard time in ministry—affirming that I handled things in the right way. This has been huge for my confidence.

Nate Sallee: Knowing that my mentor had my back was invaluable to my confidence to lead strong.

Andrew Bernardez: Every person that sits on the phone and listens to me or vent, those times of support speak volumes. I feel like I have someone on my side, rooting me on.

CHARACTERISTIC 14: HELP

"When you pass through the waters, I will be with you; and when you pass through the rivers, they will not sweep over you. When you walk through the fire, you will not be burned; the flames will not set you ablaze" (Isaiah 43:2).

When you are lost, you need help. When you are hurt, you need help. When you are confused, you need help. Every mentor needs to find out what their protégé needs and then provide the help needed to fill the gap. Ultimately, every mentor is a helper, a supplier to the needs of the protégé.

Tim Captain: The greatest impacts of mentorship has been helping me walk through life's disappointments. I watched my mentor in difficult situations. With gentleness and certainty he would try to guide the situation to a resolution. I wanted to be helped but learn to help others in tension-filled situations too. My mentor helped me be protected when I had slacked off or was ill prepared. This left me feeling guilty. The tension between experiencing the pain will move you forward and knowing that someone will be there to rescue you from a dangerous situation is just the help I needed.

Jeremy Lawson: Everyone needs someone to advise, give resources and ideas. It is invaluable.

Garrett Schrantz: Being supported and helped by my mentor has been an extremely consistent part of my life. It has meant more than I can describe and one that I can never repay except that it's a gift that I hope to use to enrich others.

Nate Sallee: I remember sitting in my office and having my mentor come in and simply ask—How can I help you? It was powerful because I knew there was substance behind it.

CHARACTERISTIC 15: LOVE

"And now these three remain: faith, hope and love. But the greatest of these is love" (1 Corinthians 13:13).

Agape love is wanting the best for the other person. In every mentoring relationship, there is a love that abides hoping the protégé will fulfill everything God has called them to become. It is the joy of the mentor to be used to make that happen.

Drew Thurman: Bob Goff wrote, "Give away time and you'll find empathy; Give away empathy and you'll find love; Give away love and you'll find purpose. Keep trading up." My mentor was willing to inconvenience himself to join us in our lives and our struggles. It was that very moment, my understanding of the love that happens in mentoring changed.

Scott Solemine: I have seen my mentor's love in my life. He genuinely cared for me. I remember a night when my character and call as a pastor was being attacked. With the little bit of energy I had left, I reached out to my mentor and he poured his love and encouragement into me. I would not have gotten through that time without him.

Garrett Schrantz: The feeling of acceptance and love no matter the mistakes I have made in the past or in the present have made all the difference. Love from my mentor is knowing that he will always be there for me even though I will not be perfect.

Tim Captain: It might sound strange but I would take a bullet for my mentor and he would take one for me. This relationship is not just about ministry and success but it's about caring deeply about each other's life. It's a gut level relationship.

Nate Sallee: Trust in my mentor is built upon a foundation that this guy loves me and wants God's best for me and my family.

Mentoring is the gift of sharing oneself with another by helping the protégé achieve all that God has placed in them. While God has been and will always be the true change agent in our lives, He uses each mentor's wisdom and experience—both good and bad—to help shape their protégé. Mentoring is the passing of the baton. It is understanding that each leader will be measured not only by what they have done in life and ministry but by those who have been taught and guided along the way. Life will be measured by those who come behind us—by those who take the leader's place. It is necessary that each leader understand their responsibility to raise up other leaders that will go higher than the mentor ever dreamed. As the Apostle Paul stated about being a nursing mother and a caring father, each mentor wants his children to accomplish more they have done. It will be the joy and fulfillment of every mentor to be represented well by their protégés!

Application Questions

1. How are you striving to maintain your integrity in your words, actions, and relationships? Why is integrity so critical to a minister's short- and long-term success? In what ways does mentoring contribute to integrity?

2. Do you recall ways that your mentors sacrificed to create margin to invest in you? What do you, or would you have to, sacrifice in order to mentor someone? To what degree does that level of sacrifice affect your interest, excitement, and follow-through? At the end of the day, are you willing to make the necessary sacrifice to invest in someone else's transformation efforts?

3. In what ways is truth a critical foundation for a productive mentoring relationship? To what degree are you truthful with people who are investing in your life and ministry, and to what degree are you undermining the process by deception, sleight of hand, or dishonesty?

4. How does prayer uniquely contribute to the mentoring process and why is it so important? How consistently are you praying for your mentor(s) and mentee(s)? What mechanisms are you using to capture, organize, and faithfully lift up prayer concerns on their behalf?

5. To what degree, and in what specific ways, are you being encouraged through your mentoring relationships? How is investing in other people contributing to your level of fulfillment? How are you being encouraged through your interactions with your mentor?

Group Discussion Questions

1. What are some examples of ways that you have received practical help from someone who was more knowledgeable, experienced, or resourced than you? In what ways and areas are you most naturally able to provide help to the people you are mentoring?

2. To what degree should you have a friendship with your mentor(s) or

protégé(s)? What are the benefits of developing a friendship with them? What are the down sides? Are there boundaries that should be put in place? If so, give some examples and explain why.

3. When looking for a mentor or mentee, how important is it to select someone with whom you have shared experiences? How do shared experiences enhance the mentoring relationship? To what degree, and in what specific ways, should a mentor and mentee continue to manufacture new shared experiences?

4. Give an example of a time when a mentor helped you believe in yourself, particularly during times that were filled with doubt. When have you helped a mentee overcome low self-esteem and achieve something that they felt was beyond reach? What are some strategies that you can use to identify doubts and fears and help your mentee achieve success?

5. On a scale of 1 (not well at all) to 10 (extremely well), how well do you normally receive correction? What are your natural reactions when someone corrects your words, performance, look, etc.? What can you do to improve how you respond to correction? In what ways can a mentor soften correction and improve the chances that the mentee hears, internalizes, and responds productively to correction?

Once we engage in personal sanctification – transformation – then we are ready to become Christ's witnesses in our neighborhoods. The manual for fulfilling Christ's mission is the book of Acts. *The Center for Church Leadership* will tackle the mission of Christ's *Ekklesia* in 2019. Here's a quick overview to whet your appetite. Luke, the author of Acts, introduces us to his neighborhood. Every type of person in Luke's neighborhood can be found in our neighborhoods today. Each neighbor has his or her own *spiritual profile*.

In the book of Acts, Luke identifies at least eleven different spiritual profiles: The Religious in Acts 2; The Hurting – The lame man in Acts 3; The Spiritualist – Simon in Acts 8; The Seeker – the Ethiopian in Acts 8; The Fanatic – Saul in Acts 9; the Good Person – Cornelius in Acts 10; The Successful – Lydia in Acts 16; the Abuser – the Philippian Jailer in Acts 16; The Skeptic – Athens in Acts 17; The Misinformed – the disciples at Ephesus in Acts 19; and The Pleasure Seeker – Felix in Acts 24. Each spiritual profile has some unique question about, distortion of, or incorrect view of God. Those questions and distortions are THE barriers that create a distrust, fear, or dislike of our heavenly Father in our unsaved neighbors. Until we understand the distortion and address it with biblical answers, our neighbors will continue to struggle to make Christ Lord and Savior.

Luke's neighbors are in your neighborhood too! And your neighbors have their own unique questions or distortion relating to God that need to be addressed. For example, before the *Hurting* will be ready to accept Christ, they may need you to answer some twisted beliefs about God's role in evil such as, "Why is God punishing me with this sickness?" and "Why doesn't God stop people from dying?" The *Skeptic* may need you to answer questions like, "How do you know there's a God?" and, "If there is a God what is he or she like?" The *Good Person* believes they can earn their salvation by being good and that Judgment Day will operate on the basis of a teeter-totter. They think that God will take all the honorable deeds and place them on one side and lay all the bad deeds on the other side. If there are more "good" deeds than "bad," the person makes it into heaven! This person needs to know that such a view is a distortion of God's justice and love. The *Successful* believe their wealth, position, and power are proof that God validates their lifestyle. They need to know that this is not necessarily true.

Here's how to work out Christ's mission in your neighborhood. *First*, build relationships with your neighbors; establish friendships. *Second*, love them; look for ways to express God's kindness through words and actions. *Third*, begin to have spiritual conversations; present questions like, "What was your family life like as you were growing up?" and, "How religious was your family when you were growing up?" One question will usually lead to another. *Fourth*, begin to craft their spiritual profile. Determine their general belief system and the corresponding questions and distortions of God that need to be address. *Fifth*, do your homework. Get some answers. "Be able to give a reason for the hope that you have" (1 Peter 3:15). Approach your neighbors with interest, love, and respect, and they will eventually be open to hearing the Good News. Then, present the gospel message that Peter delivered in Acts 2!

Alphabetically by last name . . .

ALAN AHLGRIM

Alan is the Founding Pastor of Rocky Mountain Christian Church in Niwot, CO and transitioned to become the Director of Pastor Care and Leadership Development at Blessing Ranch in Livermore, CO. He has degrees from Milligan College, B.A.; Southern Baptist Theological Seminary, Master of Divinity; and Fuller Theological Seminary, Doctor of Ministry. Alan and his wife, Linda, and have three grown children and one wonder dog, Molly.

JEFFREY DERICO

Jeffrey is a preacher's kid with a passion for Kingdom work. His educational background includes a BS in Christian Ministries, an MA in Theological Studies, and a PhD in Leadership. He served as Minister of Adult Discipleship at Indian Creek Christian Church in Indianapolis, IN and has taught at Cincinnati Christian University as an adjunct faculty member since 2004. He also serves as a board member for Center for Global Impact. He is happily married with three fantastic children who range from 15 to 7 years of age.

DAVE FAUST

Dave Faust has led churches in New York and Cincinnati, and currently serves as Associate Minister with East 91st Street Christian Church in Indianapolis. For 12 years he was president of Cincinnati Christian University. He has written several books, and for the last 22 years he has authored a weekly column for *The Lookout* magazine. He served as president of the 2006 North American Christian Convention. Dave has been married for 42 years to his wife Candy. They have three grown children, two sons-in-law, and three grandchildren.

BOB RUSSELL

God has blessed Bob Russell with a life much different than one he could have ever imagined. As a young man growing up in northern Pennsylvania, Bob had intended on becoming a high school basketball coach in his hometown. During his senior year of high school, however, Bob realized a desire in his heart to enter the ministry. Soon thereafter, he enrolled in Cincinnati Bible Seminary where he graduated in 1965.

At just twenty-two years of age, Bob became the pastor of Southeast Christian Church. That small congregation of 120 members became one of the largest churches in America, with 18,000 people attending the three worship services every weekend in 2006 when Bob retired. Now through Bob Russell Ministries, Bob continues to preach at churches and conferences throughout the United States, provide guidance for church leadership, mentor other ministers and author Bible study videos for use in small groups.

Bob and his wife Judy have two married sons, Rusty and Phil. They also have seven grandchildren with whom they enjoy spending their time. Bob also enjoys playing golf and is an avid University of Louisville football and basketball fan.

LARRY TRAVIS

Larry was called into the ministry when he was 21 years old and the journey of ministry has been incredible since. This journey has led him from youth ministry, to preaching ministry, to college professor, to college administration, and now back to the preaching ministry at Nicholson Christian Church in Independence, KY. He has been fortunate to travel to 37 countries preaching and training leaders. He enjoys mentoring students & leaders both in college and in the church.

TIM WALLINGFORD

Tim's education includes a B.S. from Cincinnati Christian University; M.A. in Apologetics, M.M. in Church Growth and M.Div. from Cincinnati Bible Seminary. Tim did doctorate studies at Southern Baptist Seminary and received his D.Min from Emmanuel School of Religion. Tim has served in the local ministry 40 years. His experience includes being the lead minister in churches ranging from 23 members as a Seminary student to 2,300 members later in life. He has served as an adjunct professor 15 years.